WORLD CLASS QUALITY

Design of Experiments Made Easier, More Cost Effective Than SPC

KEKI R. BHOTE

AMA Management Briefing

AMA MEMBERSHIP PUBLICATIONS DIVISION
AMERICAN MANAGEMENT ASSOCIATION

To my daughters,
Safeena and Shenaya,
and my sons,
Adi and Xerxes.
May they achieve
world class performance in their chosen fields.

Cover design: Shenaya Bhote-Siegel

LIBRARY OF CONGRESS
Library of Congress Cataloging-in-Publication Data

Bhote, Keki R., 1925-
    World class quality: design of experiments made easier, more cost effective
than SPC/Keki R. Bhote.
        p. cm.—(AMA management briefing)
        ISBN 0-8144-2334-5: $10.00 ($7.50 to members: $3.75 to students)
        1. Quality control—Statistical methods. 2. Process control—Statistical
methods. 3. Experimental design. I. Title. II. Series.
    TS156.B56   1988   658.5'62—dc19   88-2180   CIP

©1988 AMA Membership Publications Division

American Management Association, New York
All rights reserved. Printed in the United States of America

This Management Briefing has been distributed to all members enrolled in
the Manufacturing, Packaging, Research and Development, and Purchasing
Divisions of the American Management Association. Copies may be pur-
chased at the following single-copy rates: AMA members, $7.50. Nonmem-
bers, $10.00. Students, $3.75 (upon presentation of a college/university
identification card at an AMA bookstore). Faculty members may purchase 25
or more copies for classroom use at the student discount rate (order on college
letterhead).

Fifth Printing

Contents

Introduction

The Economic Imperative of Quality

There is a story about a man who has lost a gold coin. His friend asks him why he is looking in one area when he has said he is sure he had lost it in another. "Because the light is better here," the man replies!

The tale suggests American industry's frantic search for ways of reducing costs. It looks in the wrong places—because it is easier. Mindless layoffs, arbitrary cuts in headcounts, the flight offshore to reduce the costs of direct labor (which account for a tiny 5% of sales), and musical-chair reorganizations—all of which are easily mandated, but their effectiveness remains a mirage.

QUALITY: THE KEY TO THE MAGIC KINGDOM

Yet in this search the gold coin of quality is generally overlooked by corporations. It is seldom viewed as the most effective weapon in a company's cost-reduction arsenal. True, there has been a growing recognition of the importance of quality over the past ten years. But quality is dished out to a nervous management in portions of fear and blackmail: "Embrace quality or you will lose your business; improve reliability lest the Damocles Sword of product liability kill you; strengthen customer satisfaction if you want to avoid the ghost of Ralph Nader stalking you; and worship quality lest the Japanese eat your lunch!" The need for quality, however, is much more positive.

The famous PIMS (Profit Impact of Market Strategy) data—published by the Strategic Planning Institute after being culled from more than 3,000 businesses—indicate that as quality goes from low to high, productivity, market share, profit on sales, and return on investment also go from low to high. In this remarkable correlation, quality is the *cause,* while the other measures are the effects. Quality is the engine that can drive companies smiling all the way to the bank.

THE STAGGERING COST OF POOR QUALITY

Why is there such a huge cost-reduction bang for a modest quality buck? The answer lies in the enormous costs of poor quality— warranty, scrap, repair, analyzing, inspection and test—which range from 10% to 20% of the sales dollar. To put it more dramatically, *through poor quality each employee wastes from $100 to $200 every single day!* It is possible—no, imperative—to reduce these costs that add no value, through a comprehensive quality system. Cutting these costs, even by an easily achievable 50%, can double profits for most companies. No other cost-reduction tool can even come close.

Further, these quality costs are only those readily picked up by traditional accounting systems. They represent but the tip of the iceberg. If all the costs of poor quality that accounting is *incapable* of gathering,* such as customers switching to competitors, equipment down time, supplier delinquencies, long manufacturing and design cycle times, white-collar errors, and the poor quality of management (the largest single cause of them all) are included, the estimate could reach an astronomical 50% of the sales dollar—almost $500 per employee per day!

---

*The author has developed methods, using a new technique called the "next operation as customer" (NOAC), to tackle and reduce these intangible but insidious quality costs, along with a reflected reduction in cycle time.

THE MARCH TO WORLD-CLASS QUALITY

To move quality from the dismal levels that exist today toward world-class status requires advances on several fronts:

- Management must move from problem detection, sorting, and correction to making quality a key corporate strategy and a superordinate value that filters down to the "action quotient" of every employee.
- Organizationally, management must move from viewing quality control as the policeman to the concept of the team as the most effective building block of an organization. (Isn't it providential that teams do not appear on that bureaucratic anachronism, the organization chart?)
- The measurement system must progress beyond quality costs (80% of U.S. companies do not even know their costs of poor quality) toward 100% yields and theoretical cycle time achievement.
- Profit worship must give way to customer worship. (Forty years ahead of Japanese management, Henry Ford practiced his philosophy that if customers were truly satisfied, profits would follow). And our customer horizon should be extended to view the next operation as the customer, not as the enemy!
- Engineering designs can no longer be tossed over the wall to production. Products must be designed for maximum manufacturability and reliability, with minimum design cycle time.
- Supplier relationships can no longer be adversarial. The supplier must become a valued partner, an extension of the company.
- The worker can no longer be regarded as just a pair of hands. His brain must be tapped along with his brawn. To achieve this, managers must drive out fear, which is corrosive and unbecoming in the world's greatest democracy. Managers must mingle with their people, get involved with them, shed their bossiness and instead become teachers, coaches, and cheerleaders.

A Rubber Hammer

It is beyond the scope of this briefing to provide a blueprint for improvement in these general areas. Instead, the concentration will be on easy, simple, cost-effective—yet statistically powerful—tools. To illustrate this route of the march to world-class quality, there is a story related by Bill Conway, the former chairman of the Nashua Corporation—an early champion of statistical process control (S.P.C.) in the United States. A high-level Ford delegation had visited Nashua to discover the reasons for its quality success. Conway asked them a simple question. "Suppose I ask two of you vice-presidents to enter a contest. The winner would win a Hawaiian vacation for his whole family. I know that both of you are totally motivated and dedicated by virtue of your rise at Ford. The contest is to see who can drive a nail into this wall. One of you will get a hammer, the other nothing but his management encouragement. Who do you think will win!" The answer was obvious. Motivation, important as it may be, is not enough. People at all levels must have tools. But they must be the right tools for the right job. *Unfortunately, what passes for statistical process control (S.P.C.) in this country is a rubber hammer—weak, cumbersome, and obsolete.*

BRIEFING OBJECTIVES

The objectives of this briefing are:

- To describe in simple, *nonmathematical* terms a variety of easy, but statistically powerful, techniques that can be learned and practiced by all levels in a company—from managers and engineers to technicians and line workers. The emphasis will be on the practical, doable method.
- To show how it is possible to progress from the current unacceptably high defect rates to zero defects, and from zero defects to zero variation, through the use of simple designed experiments, and to achieve this objective coupled with substantially reduced costs.
- To urge the replacement of ineffective control charts that, unfortunately, appear to enjoy a popularity of band-wagon dimensions, with precontrol, which is simpler, less costly, and more effective.

TANGIBLE BENEFITS

The benefits to those who can implement these techniques—and, fortunately, a few thousand practitioners already have—are:

- The elimination of high scrap and rework—and on to zero failures and 100% yields.
- Drastic reduction of inspection and tests that are non-value-added operations.
- The virtual elimination of unplanned equipment or process down time.
- The appreciable reduction in manufacturing cycle time, because quality improvement is a prerequisite to the shortening of cycle time.
- Improved employee morale—since success breeds success—instead of the hit-and-miss practices and mixed results of quality circles.
- The doubling of profits through a systematic reduction in the costs of poor quality.
- The ability to leapfrog the Japanese in the use of powerful quality tools.

METHODOLOGY

Part I of this briefing starts with an outline of elementary S.P.C. tools so as to provide a background for the even simpler, yet more effective, tools discussed later. There is a comparison between the complexity and weakness of control charts and the simplicity and cost effectiveness of the newer tool of precontrol. Finally, parameters to measure variation—C_p and C_{pk}—are developed, along with a treatment of the sources of variation and the general methods used to reduce it.

Part II concentrates on the design of experiments—the principal weapons to go beyond zero defects and 100% yields to the promised land of zero variation. The seven weapons are: multi-vari charts, components search, paired comparisons, variables search, full factorials, B vs. C, and scatter plots. The most forbidding aspect of these weapons are their names! From that point on, it's all downhill! Each technique is explained in an easy, nonmathematical, nontheoretical manner, with a case study and a practice exercise given to guide the reader in implementing each method with almost immediate results.

Part III returns to the true role of S.P.C. as a maintenance—not a problem-solving—technique, and to the steps that should be taken to assure its effectiveness. Finally, there is a prescription for companies on how to marshal their resources for best designing experiments and S.P.C. implementation in order to achieve world-class quality.

Part I:

Traditional Statistical Process Control (S.P.C.)

Chapter 1

Elementary S.P.C. Tools

This chapter will briefly outline elementary statistical process control (S.P.C.) tools that have long been used in Japan and are now beginning to be put into practice in the United States. Before describing them, however, it maybe useful to survey the contrasting approaches to quality taken by Japan and the United States.

JAPANESE vs. U.S. QUALITY: CONTRASTING TECHNIQUES

Figure 1 compares relative quality progress in Japan and the United States. Following World War II, U.S. quality reigned supreme, but Japan achieved parity by the late 1960s and has widened the gap in its favor ever since. The contrast becomes even starker when three major techniques to achieve quality—the traditional approach, S.P.C., and the design of experiments (D.O.E.)—are examined. Traditional quality control consists of ineffective methods such as brute-force inspection, management exhortation, delegation of quality responsibility to a detached quality control department, and even sampling plans. As seen in Figure 1, Japan abandoned this kindergarten approach as early as the 1960s, whereas the United States persevered with such obsolete tools well into the early 1980s.

Figure 1. The contribution of traditional, S.P.C. and D.O.E. tools to quality progress.

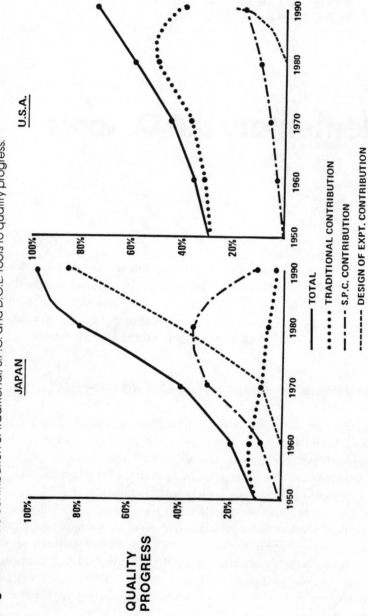

TOTAL
TRADITIONAL CONTRIBUTION
S.P.C. CONTRIBUTION
DESIGN OF EXPT. CONTRIBUTION

JAPAN

U.S.A.

QUALITY
PROGRESS

S.P.C. in Japan—"Too Little and Too Late"

As a result of W. Edwards Deming, Joseph M. Juran, and other U.S. trainers,* Japan launched S.P.C. in the 1950s and rode its crest till the mid-1970s, when it concluded that S.P.C. in production was too little and too late. Ironically, just as Japan was discarding S.P.C., especially for its professionals, America was rediscovering it! (S.P.C. had been used in the United States during World War II, but the baby was thrown out with the bath water in a revolt against the mysteries of the world of statistics.)

"If Japan Can, Why Can't We?"

What reushered in the S.P.C. age in America was the airing of the NBC White Paper "If Japan Can, Why Can't We?" It gave the American public at large its first glimpse of the reasons behind Japan's success—quality, in general, and S.P.C., in particular. Deming was rescued from the U.S. industrial wilderness and elevated as a prophet within his own country. Major companies scurried to jump on the S.P.C. bandwagon. Unfortunately for the United States, S.P.C. has become synonymous with control charts. As we shall see later, control charts are complex, costly, and almost useless in their ability to solve chronic quality problems.

DESIGN OF EXPERIMENTS: JAPAN'S SECRET WEAPON

The central thrust, and secret weapon, of Japanese quality is its widespread use of design of experiments (D.O.E.). The object of D.O.E. is to discover key variables in product and process design, to drastically reduce the variations they cause, and to open up the tolerances on the lesser variables so as to reduce costs. Figure 1 shows the spectacular rise in the use of D.O.E., especially since 1970. Hundreds of Japanese companies conduct thousands of these designed experiments each year to make product and process designs "more robust." The discipline is a variant of the classical design of

*The author has played a role in the quality training of his company's Japanese joint venture as well as in that of Japanese suppliers. Some of his publications have been translated into Japanese and circulated by the Japanese Union of Scientists and Engineers.

experiments founded by Sir Ronald Fisher of Britain seventy years ago. The principal Japanese D.O.E. architect is Dr. Genichi Taguchi, who adapted the classical methods into his system of "orthogonal arrays."

In the United States, by contrast, D.O.E. was practically unheard of until the 1980s, except by a small band of academics and missionary statisticians. But a belated movement is now under way. Mesmerized by the Taguchi name, American business has imported his methods wholesale. Its irrational logic is: "If it is Japanese, it has to be good!" However, as we shall see later, this Japanese mystique is complicated, expensive, time-consuming, and statistically flawed.

S.P.C. TOOLS FOR JAPANESE LINE WORKERS

Although the Japanese abandoned S.P.C. tools for the more powerful D.O.E. techniques, there are two exceptions—one minor, the other major. The minor exception is that they still trot out control charts as show-and-tell for visiting American firemen, so that their advanced D.O.E. methods can escape the scrutiny of fact-finding delegations! The major exception is that they have trained their entire direct labor force in elementary S.P.C. tools, so that they can tackle low-grade quality problems through their quality circles, *Kaizen* (improvement) teams, and employee suggestions.* The result? Instead of having a few professionals to tackle problems, they now have a whole host, albeit low-grade, of problem solvers.

Table 1 lists these elementary S.P.C. techniques—often called the seven tools of Q.C.—that every Japanese line worker learns and uses. Because they are both limited in value as well as explained in many texts on the subject of quality control, only the objectives and methodology are outlined here. The one exception is the control chart, which will be discussed in some detail in the next chapter. A brief commentary on each of these tools is in order.

---

*The number of suggestions turned in by Japanese workers is legendary. Whereas the average number of suggestions per employee per year in the United States is 0.1, the figure in Japan is over 10. In Japanese companies that directly compete with American firms, the number is closer to 50. More important, over 80% of these worker suggestions are approved by Japanese management. The quality circles experiment with their own ideas, try pilot-runs, and submit their suggestions to management only when they are sure of success. Management approval then becomes almost automatic.

Table 1. Elementary S.P.C. tools.

TOOL	OBJECTIVE	METHODOLOGY	WHEN TO USE	TYPICAL USERS
1. PDCA (<u>P</u>lan, <u>D</u>o, <u>C</u>heck, <u>A</u>ct)	Problem-solve by trial and error	Plan the work; execute; check results; take action if there is a deviation between desired and actual results. Repeat the cycle time till deviation is reduced to zero.	When more powerful tools unknown	Mostly line workers
2. Data Collection and Analysis	• Assess Quality • Control a Product • Regulate a Process • Accept/reject Product • Interpret Observations	Define specific reason for collecting data; decide on msmt. criteria (attribute vs. variable vs. rank); assure accuracy of measuring equipment (min. 5 times greater than product requirement); randomize; stratify data collection (time, material, machine, operator, type and location of defects) analyze data using several S.P.C., D.O.E. tools.	At All Times	Universal
3. Graphs/Charts	• Display Trends • Condense Data • Explain to Others	Select 2 or more parameters to be displayed; determine method of display (bar, line, or circle graphs are the most common); select the most appropriate scales of the parameters for maximum visual impact.	At All Times	Universal
4. •Check Sheets	• Transform raw data into categories	• Determine categories into which data is subdivided (e.g., types of defects, location of defects, days in the week, etc.). Enter quantities in each category.	In preparation for a Histogram or Frequency Distribution	Universal
•Tally Sheets	Groups, Cells in semi-pictorial fashion	• For tally sheets, divide variable being recorded into 10 levels or cells. Plot cell boundaries or mid-points. Make tally (with slash marks) of the number of observations in each cell.		

TOOL	OBJECTIVE	METHODOLOGY	WHEN TO USE	TYPICAL USERS
• Histograms/ Frequency Distri- bution	• Translate data into a picture of the average and spread of a quality characteris- tic	• Convert tally sheet data into bar graph (Histograms) or line graphs (Frequency Distributions) showing the relationship between various values of a quality characteristic and the number of obser- vations (or percentage of the total) in each value.	For Process Capability Studies in pre-produc- tion or production	Engineers, Technicians, Line workers
5. Pareto's Law	Separate the vital few causes of a problem or effect from the trivial many. Concent- rate attention on former.	• Identify as many causes of a problem and the contribution of each to a given effect ($, percentages, etc.), plot causes on X-axis, effects (cumlative) on Y-axis in ascending or descending order of magnitude. Prioritize action on those few causes that account for most of the effect (generally, 20% or less of causes contribute 80% or more of effect)	At All Times	Universal- A fantastic tool for prioritization in Mfg. or white collar work
6. Brain- storming	Generate as many ideas to solve a problem or improve a process, utilizing synergistic power of a group	Gather a group most concerned with problem; define problem precisely; ask each member to write down cause of problem or improvement ideas; then, open the floor for an outpouring of ideas, rational or irrational; no criticisms allowed; record ideas; narrow down the most worthwhile ideas.	• Initial Problem- Solving • "Process" Improve- ment	• Quality Circles, • Improvement teams

Technique	Purpose	Description		Users
• Cause & Effect (Ishikawa; fishbone diagram)	• Organize problem causes into main groups and sub-groups in order to have total visibility of all causes and determine where to start corrective action	• Define the problem; construct a "fishbone" diagram with the major causes (e.g., material, machine, method and man) as the main "branches" and add detailed causes within each main cause as "twigs". Quantify the spec. limits established for each cause where possible, the actual value measured for each cause and its effect upon the problem. If a relationship between cause and effect can be shown quantitatively draw a box around the cause. If the relationship is difficult to quantify, underline the cause. If there is no proof that a cause is related to the effect, do not mark the cause. Prioritize the most important causes with a circle. Experiment with these in PDCA fashion until root cause is located.		
• CEDAC Cause & Effect Diagram with the Addition of Cards	Same as Cause & Effect Diagram & earlier Identification of causes & better worker participation	Workers, at their individual workplaces, identify causes on the spot as they occur. Cards, used to identify such causes can then be readily changed by the workers.	Same as Cause & Effect Diagram	Same as Cause & Effect Diagram
7. Control Charts	Maintain a parameter with minimum variation after major causes have been captured & reduced	DETAILED IN NEXT CHAPTER	• Not for problem-solving. • Production	Engineers, Technicians, Line workers

1. **P.D.C.A.** (Plan, Do, Check, Act). Allegedly taught by Deming, the P.D.C.A. cycle has recently been claimed as a Japanese innovation. It is a variant of the traditional problem-solving approach of "observe, think, try, explain." As a problem-solving tool, it has the same poor effectiveness as brainstorming and Kepner-Tragoe detective techniques for solving technical problems.

2. **Data Collection and Analysis.** This is the first step in the long road to variation identification and reduction. Sound planning is the key to effective data collection. The "why, what, when, where, who, and how" of data must be established *a priori*, i.e., before the fact. This avoids teams and plants drowning in meaningless and useless data. Common pitfalls include: not defining the objective; not knowing what parameter to measure or how to measure it; not having sufficiently accurate equipment for the measurement; not randomizing (a fundamental statistical flaw in Taguchi's design of experiments); and poor stratification of data. Similarly, the analysis of data should be undertaken only with proven approaches (many of these are detailed in later chapters of this briefing) rather than with hit-and-miss approaches, such as P.D.C.A., brainstorming, cause-and-effect diagrams, etc.

3. **Graphs/Charts.** These are tools for the organization, summarization, and statistical display of data. As in the case of data collection and analysis, the purpose of using graphs and charts should be clearly established and their usefulness and longevity periodically reexamined.

4. **Check Sheets/Tally Sheets/Histograms/Frequency Distributions.** There are several types of check sheets—for process distribution; for defective items/causes/defect locations (sometimes referred to as "measles charts"); and as memory joggers for inspectors, quality control, and servicers in checking product. Their main function is to simplify data gathering and to arrange data for statistical interpretation and analysis.

Tally sheets are special forms of check sheets to record data, keep score of a process in operation, and divide data into distinct groups to facilitate statistical interpretation.

Histograms and frequency distributions provide a graphical portrayal of variability. Their shape often gives clues about the process measured, such as mixed lots (bimodal distribution); screened lots (truncated distribution); amount of spread relative to specifications; noncentered spread relative to specifications, etc. There are two general characteristics of frequency distributions that can be quantified—central tendency and dispersion. Central tendency is the bunching-up effect of observations of a particular quality characteristic near the center and can be measured by average ($\overline{X}$) of all the observations, mode (the value of a quality characteristic with the largest number of observations), and median (the value that divides the number of observations into two equal parts). Dispersion is the spread of the observations and can be measured by range (R)—i.e., the highest observation minus the lowest—and standard deviation, which is approximately one-sixth of range (but only for a normal distribution).

5. Pareto's Law. Vilfredo Federico Pareto was a nineteenth-century Italian economist who studied the distribution of income in Italy and concluded that a very limited number of people owned most of its wealth. The study produced the famous Pareto-Lorenz mal-distribution law, which states that cause and effect are not linearly related; that a few causes produce most of a given effect; and, more specifically, that 20% or less of causes produce 80% or more of effects.

Juran, however, is credited with converting Pareto's law into a versatile, universal industrial tool applicable in diverse areas, such as quality, manufacturing, suppliers, materials, inventory control, cycle time, value engineering, sales and marketing—in fact, in any industrial situation—blue-collar or white-collar. By separating the few important causes of any industrial phenomenon from the trivial many, work on the few causes can be prioritized. Figure 2 is a typical example of a Pareto chart and its usefulness. Three items, which alone accounted for $2,800 per month of loss (or over 80% of the total loss) in (a), were prioritized and reduced to $1,400 per month in (b), before the remaining problems were tackled.

6. Brainstorming/Cause and Effect Diagrams/CEDAC. Brainstorming is a good example of a beautiful technique applied wrongly. In the social sciences, and even in white-collar industrial work, it is a marvelous tool for generating and stimulating the maximum number of ideas, utilizing group synergy. In fact, in value engineering (V.E.), it is an essential element of the V.E. job plan. However, its effectiveness in quality problem solving is highly

Figure 2. Examples of Pareto chart before and after improvement.

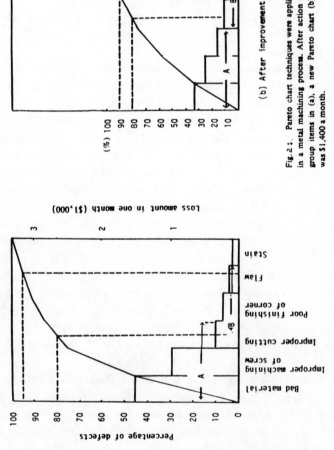

Loss amount in one month ($1,000)

(b) After improvement

Fig. 2 : . Pareto chart techniques were applied to reduce losses generated in a metal machining process. After action has been taken to improve A group items in (a), a new Pareto chart (b) was prepared. Total saving was $1,400 a month.

Loss amount in one month ($1,000)

Percentage of defects

Bad material

Improper machining of screw

Improper cutting

Poor finishing of corner

Flaw

Stain

(a) Before Improvement

overrated. Even though group ideas are generally better than individual ones, guessing at problems is a kindergarten approach to finding the root cause of variation.

Cause-and-effect diagrams were developed by Dr. Kaoru Ishikawa, one of the foremost authorities on quality control in Japan. As a result, it is often called the Ishikawa diagram or, by reason of its shape, a fishbone diagram. It is probably the most widely used quality control tool for problem solving among blue-collar workers in Japan. However, its effectiveness is poor. At best, it is like playing Russian roulette. At worst, its success probabilities are not much better than the odds in Las Vegas. It is a hit-and-miss process in which finding the solution can take months or even years. Often, because only one cause is varied at a time, interaction effects (explained later) are missed, which results in partial solutions and marginal improvement in quality. Yet it has a few redeeming features.

Figure 3 is an example of a cause-and-effect diagram, listing all the possible causes that can produce solder defects in a wave solder process. (For the sake of simplicity, only two major branches—machine and machine materials—are shown. For a complete picture, board and electronic component branches should be added to the chart.) Figure 3 is an excellent compilation of all the variables that can cause a solder defect. It also highlights—with circles—those variables judged to be important. In more complex charts, the specification limits and the observed variations from these limits would be recorded for each cause. Such observations, if carefully recorded, can provide some leads in problem solving. In the final analysis, however, guesses, hunches, opinions, and engineering judgment are crude problem-solving tools. Instead, as the great Dorian Shainin* suggests: "Talk to the parts, they are smarter than the engineers." What he means by this is that the parts contain all the

*Dorian Shainin is one of the "gurus" of quality on the American scene. Among the others, Phil Crosby is the showman, useful for companies in the dark ages of quality. Juran is superb for general quality management. Deming now concentrates on twisting top management's tail. Shainin alone is the consummate "tool" man—the master problem solver. Shainin is a portly man. But unlike the Aga Khan, who was weighed in gold and, later, in diamonds, Shainin is truly worth his weight in both gold and diamonds for his tremendous contribution to S.P.C. and the design of the experiments. Techniques like the lot plot plan, precontrol, multi-vari charts, components search, paired companies, and variables search were either invented by him or forged into sledgehammer power by his adaptations of earlier developments. This author is an unabashed disciple of Dorian Shainin and is deeply grateful to this great American for his tutelage.

Figure 3. Cause and effect diagram.

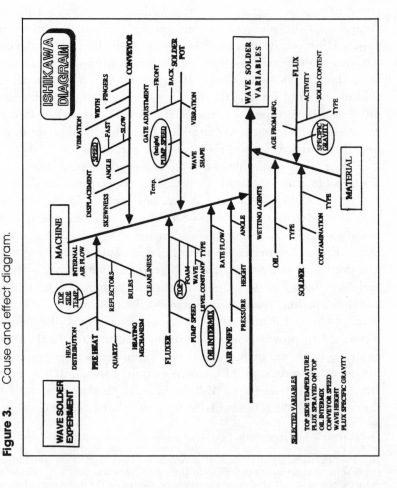

information on problem causes and variation, and that their secrets can be unlocked through appropriate statistically designed experiments.

CEDAC is the acronym for *cause* and *effect* *diagram* with the *addition* of *cards*. Developed by Ryuji Fukuda, another noted Japanese authority, the technique is explained in detail in his book *Managerial-Engineering*, published by Productivity, Inc. CEDAC represents an improvement over the cause-and-effect diagram, with workers free to change any "branch or twig" cause in the diagram as they observe new phenomena in a process and thereby gain new insights. The use of cards, under their own control, facilitates such instant updating of causes. Worker participation is enhanced and raw, nonquantifiable information is captured before it "evaporates" in tedious data gathering. Yet CEDAC suffers from the same judgment weaknesses that cause-and-effect diagrams contain.

7. Control Charts. The last of the elementary "seven tools of Q.C." is the control chart. Because of its wide use and misuse, a good portion of the next chapter will be devoted to it.

Chapter 2

Control Charts vs. Precontrol: Horse and Buggy vs. the Jet Age

In the minds of many, quality professionals and nonprofessionals alike, the control chart is synonymous with statistical process control. For a number of years it held center stage in the discipline that used to be called statistical quality control. The American Society for Quality Control still uses the chart as its emblem.

THE ROLLER COASTER HISTORY OF CONTROL CHARTS

Developed by Dr. Walter Shewhart sixty years ago, the control chart quickly became a bridge between the academic world of the laboratory and the hard-headed world of production. In the post-World War II period, however, as walls got plastered with control charts, their usefulness began to be challenged. No tools had been developed to tackle out-of-control conditions—not even simple tools, such as brainstorming and cause-and-effect diagrams. Once disillusionment set in, the control chart was banished.

By the late 1970s, however, America's industrial lead had vanished and its invulnerability stood exposed as a myth. The Japanese challenge evoked an intensive search for the key to quality. S.P.C. seemed to be that key. NBC's documentary "If Japan Can, Why Can't We?" became the continental divide between a pre-S.P.C. and post-S.P.C. era. The control chart was recalled from exile and received a coronation. Its reign continues. It has been a tyrannical reign, with several original equipment manufacturers (OEM) customers—especially some of the automotive companies—demanding use of the control chart as a passport to doing business with them. They force control charts down the throats of unknowing or unwilling suppliers, and bludgeon into submission those knowledgeable suppliers who dare point out that the control chart emperor wears no clothes! And, as often happens, the royal court is filled with camp followers, hangers-on, and charlatans who exploit the desperation of companies to gain a foothold on the S.P.C. bandwagon by offering courses, tutorials, consultations, and ubiquitous computer software programs—all dealing with the power and glory of control charts. Yet quality progress, as measured by C_p & C_{pk} (examined in detail in Chapter 3), has barely inched forward in the majority of American companies, despite the widespread use of control charts. In nontechnical terms, it means that the reduction of variation—an urgent overall quality goal—has hardly made any progress. Sooner or later, as statistical literacy is increased, disillusionment will once again set in and control charts will become obsolete, as they already are in Japan.

A MAINTENANCE TOOL, AT BEST

This critique of control charts does not mean that they serve no useful purpose whatsoever. *Their main function, past and present, is to maintain a process under control, once its inherent variation has been reduced through the design of experiments.* The key word here is *maintain.* The most common misuse of control charts is to put them into effect in order to solve a problem. If there is a known problem, the application of control charts will not solve it. They will simply confirm that a problem exists—making control charting redundant. A second misuse is to introduce a control chart without any prior knowledge of whether process capability exists or not. In this case, the control chart may give the answer—but only a day or two later, after 80 to 150 readings have been taken and trial control limits calculated. As we shall see later in this chapter, the technique of precontrol is a simpler and more cost-effective maintenance tool than is a control chart, and it can gauge process capability in one hundredth the time taken by the latter.

ADVANTAGES OVER FREQUENCY DISTRIBUTIONS

Frequency distributions, although they can translate masses of data into a neat picture and can provide clues about a process, have two limitations. First, they are static because they do not capture variations with time. Second, they cannot distinguish between small, random variations caused by a large number of factors—referred to as unassignable causes—and large, nonrandom variations caused by a small number of assignable factors. A control chart overcomes these obstacles. It adds the important time dimension, so that trends with time can be spotted, and it separates—in a vague way—the effects of unassignable causes that require no corrective action from the assignable causes that must be investigated and corrected.

THE MECHANICS OF CONTROL CHARTS FOR VARIABLES ($\overline{X}$ AND R CHARTS)

A full treatment of control chart practices could fill an entire book. Since there is a huge volume of published materials—texts, video-tapes, and computer programs—on control charts, it is assumed that most readers have some familiarity with them. In this briefing, only a few highlights are examined in order to compare control charts and precontrol.

Table 2 is a step-by-step procedure for generating control charts for use with variables data (i.e., where there are scalar measurements that are continuously variable, such as dimensions, weights, voltages, temperatures, speeds, etc.).

Table 2.   Trial control chart procedure.

1. Select key product parameter(s) from the process to be controlled, based on importance/jeopardy.
2. Take periodic samples (say, every ½ hr., or 1 hr., etc.) from the process with a subgroup size of, say, 4 or 5 units in each sample.
3. Run the process to obtain a minimum of 25 to 30 such samples.
4. For each subgroup, calculate average, $\overline{X}$, and range, R.
5. Calculate grand average, $\overline{\overline{X}}$, of all subgroup averages and calculate average range, $\overline{R}$, of all subgroup ranges.
6. Calculate upper control limit ($UCL_{\overline{X}}$) and lower control limit ($LCL_{\overline{X}}$) for $\overline{X}$ chart:

   $UCL_{\overline{X}} = \overline{\overline{X}} + A_2\overline{R}$ (See tables for A_2 values of appropriate
   $LCL_{\overline{X}} = \overline{\overline{X}} - A_2\overline{R}$ subgroup sizes)

7. Calculate upper control limit (UCL_R) and lower control limit (LCL_R) for R chart:

   $UCL_R = D_4\overline{R}$ (See tables for D_4 and D_3 values of appro-
   $LCL_R = D_3\overline{R}$ priate subgroup sizes)

8. Plot $\overline{X}$ and R charts. Draw in the control limits for $\overline{X}$ and R. If all $\overline{X}$ and R points (for each subgroup) are within their respective control limits, the process is considered stable—a constant cause system.
9. If one or more $\overline{X}$ or R points fall outside their respective control limits, use statistical problem-solving methods to find assignable causes.

Table 3 lists the formulas for calculating the upper and lower control limits for $\overline{X}$ and R charts, as well as for the most common of the attribute charts—p and c charts. (Attributes, as contrasted with variables, are discrete numbers associated with accept-reject; pass-fail; go-no-go criteria). In addition, the table provides important formulas for calculating the upper and lower limits of individual values likely from the process. This is an important step that most control chart practitioners do not even know about, much less use.

THEORETICAL UNDERPINNING FOR CONTROL CHARTS

Control chart theory is based upon the central limit theorem in statistics. This states that when subgroups—or samples—are periodi-

Table 3.   Control chart formulas.

Chart	Central Line	Lower Control Limit	Upper Control Limit
$\overline{X}$	$\overline{\overline{X}}$	$\overline{\overline{X}} - A_2\,\overline{R}$	$\overline{\overline{X}} + A_2\,\overline{R}$
R	R	$D_3\,R$	$D_4\,R$
% Defective: p	$\overline{P}$	$\overline{P} - 3\sqrt{\dfrac{\overline{p}\,(1\text{-}\overline{p})}{n}}$	$\overline{p} + 3\sqrt{\dfrac{\overline{p}\,(1\text{-}\overline{p})}{n}}$
No. of Defective: c	$\overline{c}$	$\overline{c} - 3\dfrac{\sqrt{\overline{c}}}{n}$	$\overline{c} + 3\dfrac{\sqrt{\overline{c}}}{n}$

PROCESS LIMITS

Upper Process Limit $\qquad \overline{\overline{X}} + 3\,\overline{R}/d_2*$
Lower Process Limit $\qquad \overline{\overline{X}} - 3\,\overline{R}/d_2$
*σPopulation = $\sigma^1 = \overline{R}/d_2$

Subgroup Size n	A_2	D_3	D_4	d_2
4	0.73	0	2.28	2.059
5	0.58	0	2.11	2.326

cally drawn from a process and the average of each subgroup calculated, these averages will form a normal distribution, regardless of the distribution of the individual readings of the process—or parent population. In other words, the individual readings in the process may have a non-normal, skewed, and even a discontinuous distribution. But subgroup averages drawn from any such process will be normally distributed and the algorithms of the normal distribution can be applied. The most important of these algorithms is as follows: the area under a normal curve bounded by two lines that are three standard deviations on either side of the average is 99.73% of the total area in the normal distribution. A shorthand description is that the area within $\overline{X} \pm 3\,\sigma$ of a normal distribution is 99.73%, where $\overline{X}$ is the average and σ is the Greek symbol for standard deviation—a measure of spread.

In control charts for $\overline{X}$, when subgroup averages are calculated, the derived upper and lower control limits represent the $\overline{X} \pm 3\,\sigma$ limits of the subgroup averages. Hence, if any subgroup average, $\overline{X}$, falls outside these limits, there is a (1 - 99.73%), i.e., 0.27% probability, that this average reading occurred entirely by chance, but a 99.73% confidence that it was caused by a nonrandom, assignable cause. The process must be stopped and an investigation begun to correct the problem. On the other hand, even if there is considerable variation among the $\overline{X}$ readings, but they fall within the upper and lower control limits, the variation is due to small, random, unassignable causes that are not worth investigating, and the process should be left alone.

TWO CASE STUDIES HIGHLIGHTING THE WEAKNESSES OF CONTROL CHARTS

Theoretical models, however, do not always neatly fit real-life situations. The several weaknesses of control charts are best illustrated by two case studies.

Control Charting a Bushing Parameter

In a machine shop operation, a bushing had to be made to a length of 0.500 inches $\pm$ 0.002 inches—a typical requirement. Table 4 shows the data of subgroups of five units, drawn from the process every hour on the hour. From the recorded data, the average, $\overline{X}$, and the range, R, are calculated for each subgroup. From the several $\overline{X}$ and R values, the grand average, $\overline{\overline{X}}$, and the average range, $\overline{R}$, are derived. The formulas for the upper and lower control limits shown in Table 3 are then used to compute these limits for both the $\overline{X}$ and R charts.

The results are drawn in Figure 4. It clearly shows that all subgroup averages, $\overline{X}$, are within the upper and lower control limits in the $\overline{X}$ chart. Similarly, all the subgroups, R, are within the upper and lower control limits for the R chart. This indicates that the trial control chart—which, incidentally, took one and a half shifts and many readings to complete—has established that the process is stable (otherwise called a constant cause system in statistical parlance). Process capability is now assured and full production can go forward, supposedly to fabricate thousands and thousands of units.

Table 4. Typical control chart data.

Bushing Length
Specification .500" ± .002"

Sample #	8 am	9	10	11	12 pm	1	2	3	4	5	6	7 pm
1	.501"	.501"	.502"	.501"	.501"	.500"	.500"	.500"	.501"	.502"	.501"	.500"
2	.501"	.501"	.502"	.502"	.501"	.500"	.501"	.501"	.501"	.502"	.502"	.500"
3	.500"	.501"	.502"	.501"	.501"	.502"	.501"	.501"	.501"	.502"	.501"	.501"
4	.501"	.501"	.501"	.500"	.501"	.502"	.501"	.501"	.501"	.502"	.501"	.502"
5	.502"	.502"	.501"	.500"	.501"	.502"	.500"	.500"	.501"	.501"	.501"	.501"
Sum of "X"s	2.505"	2.506"	2.507"	2.504"	2.505"	2.506"	2.505"	2.503"	2.505"	2.508"	2.506"	2.504"
$\overline{X}_1$	.501"	.5012"	.5014"	.5000"	.5010"	.5012"	.5010"	.5006"	.5006"	.5012"	.5012"	.5008"
R_1	.002"	.001"	.001"	.002"	.000"	.002"	.002"	.001"	.000"	.001"	.001"	.002"

Sum of $\overline{X}_1$ = 6.0128

Sum of R_1 = .0115

$$\overline{\overline{X}} = \frac{\Sigma \overline{X}}{N} = \frac{6.0128}{12} = .50107$$

$$\overline{R} = \frac{\Sigma R}{N} = \frac{.015}{12} = .00125$$

Control Limits:

For Sample Averages:

$$\overline{\overline{X}} \pm A_2 R = .50107 \pm (.58)(.00125)$$

UCL = .50180
LCL = .50034

For Range:

$$\overline{X} \pm A_2 R = .50107 \pm (.58)(.00125) = .00264$$

$$UCL = D_4 R = (2.11)(.00125) = .00264$$

$$LCL = D_3 R = (0)(.00125) = 0$$

Figure 4. Bushing length: $\overline{X}$ and R charts.

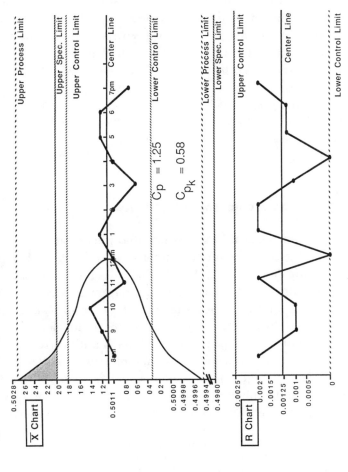

Yet if specification limits* are drawn, as shown in Figure 4, it can be seen that the upper control limit for *averages* is dangerously close to the upper specification limit for *individual readings*. Even without much statistical sophistication, any layman can reason that if average values are close to a limit, the individual values that make up the average can go beyond that limit. More precisely, the projected spread of individual values can be calculated by the formulas shown in Table 3 for process limits.** Figure 4 depicts these process limits. The upper process limit is 0.007″ above the upper specification limit, indicating that 7% to 10% of the bushings are likely to be defective. *So, here is a control chart indicating that all is well and that production should continue full speed ahead, when, in actuality, the process is likely to produce a totally unacceptable rate of defective parts!* In quality control literature, this is referred to as a β risk—the risk of accepting product that should be rejected. In this case, the β risk is at least 7%.***

Control Chart of a Sensor Capacitance

An electronic element, for sensing atmospheric pressure in an automobile, has a capacitance requirement in the range of 31 to 45 picofarads (pf). Figure 5 shows $\overline{X}$ and R control charts for the process.

In contrast to the first case study, both the $\overline{X}$ and R charts show several average and range readings outside the upper and lower control limits. The inference is that the process is hopelessly out of control and must be stopped dead in its tracks until corrected. Yet production claimed that it had produced hundreds, even thousands, of units without a single reject! To some extent, this can be seen from the raw data in the subgroups, where no individual reading is even close to either the upper or lower specification limits of 45 and 31 pf.

---

*Many control chart purists do not allow specification limits to be shown on control charts, because they believe that such a practice inhibits the necessity for continuous process improvement, which somehow, almost magically, they believe, can be achieved with control charts!

**Again, in most control chart work, process limits are not even known, much less calculated or used to gauge process capability.

***If the concept of C_p and C_{pk}, explained in Chapter 3, is used to calculate process capability, this particular process has a poor C_p of 1.25 and a totally unacceptable C_{pk} of 0.58. What a dramatic condemnation of control charts!

Further, the projected process limits for individual readings are 39.5 and 35 pf, well within the specification limit. (The projected process spread is slightly narrower than the spread of actual individual readings because the chosen subgroup size of ten was unusually large.)

Here we have the opposite condition from the one shown in the first case study—a control chart declaring that the process should be shut down, when production should in fact continue.* (On a long-term basis, the inherent variation depicted in the process can be reduced, but there is no need to stop production, as indicated by the control chart.) In quality control literature, this condition is called an α risk—i.e., the risk of rejecting a product that should be accepted.

THE DISCOVERY OF PRECONTROL

Precontrol was developed by the consulting company of Rath and Strong for a major *Fortune* 500 company that had become disenchanted with cumbersome and ineffective control charts. Precontrol's founder, Frank Satherwaite, is a brilliant statistician who established its theoretical underpinnings in a comprehensive paper thirty years ago. Unfortunately, just as precontrol was gaining recognition, America, flushed with its economic success in the post-World War II years, threw out all statistical methods in industry, control charts and precontrol included. Then, as S.P.C. became fashionable again in the 1980s and the control chart became its centerpiece, precontrol started to reappear on the statistical horizon. Two or three years ago, the ratio of control chart users to precontrol practitioners was 99:1. Today the ratio is 90:10. In a few years, as the simplicity and effectiveness of precontrol is better publicized, the control chart will be relegated to history—as in Japan—and precontrol will become the principal maintenance tool in the S.P.C. world.

THE MECHANICS OF PRECONTROL IN FOUR EASY STEPS

The mechanics of precontrol can be taught to anybody in industry,

---

*The process capability for this second case is a respectable C_p of 2.0 and a very acceptable C_{p_k} of 1.92. (See Chapter 3 for calculation of C_p and C_{p_k}.)

Figure 5.   Sensor: $\bar{X}$ and R charts.

Spec: 31 to 45 P.F.

$\bar{\bar{X}} = 37.2$ P.F. ; $\bar{R} = 2.2$; $UCL_{\bar{X}} = 37.88$; $LCL_{\bar{X}} = 36.52$; $UCL_R = 3.95$; $LCL_R = 0$

Upper Process Limit = 35.0;   Lower Process Limit = 39.5

$C_P = 2.0$; $K = 0.04$; $C_{P_K} = 1.92$

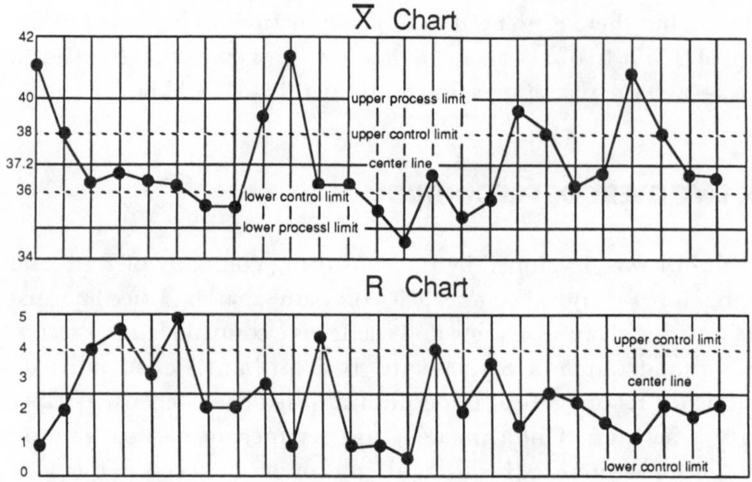

$\bar{X}$ Chart

R Chart

Sub-Group	1	2	3	4	5	6	7	8	9	10	11	12	13	14	15	16	17	18	19	20	21	22	23	24
1	40.5	37.5	36.5	38.5	38	39	37	36	38	41.5	36	37	35.5	35	39	36.5	37	39	39.5	37.5	38	40.5	39.5	38
2	40	36.5	38.5	39	37	38	36	37	39	40.5	34	36	36	34.5	38	35	38	38	39	37.5	37	40.5	37.5	37
3	39.5	38.5	37.5	36	37.5	36.5	35	35.5	38.5	41	38.5	36.5	35	34.5	37	34.5	35	38	38.5	36	36.5	40.5	37.5	36.5
4	40	38.5	35.5	39	35	38	35.5	35	38	37	35	35	35	35	34.5	39	37.5	36	36.5	40	37.5	36.5	37.5	36.5
5	39.5	38.5	34.5	34.5	35	35	36.5	36.5	39	40.5	37	36	36	34.5	36	35.5	35	39.5	37	35.5	37	41	38	37
6	40.5	38.5	36.5	34.5	35.5	34	35	35	36.5	41	37.5	36.5	36	34.5	36.5	35	36	38	37	35.5	36.5	41	38	36.5
7	40	37.5	37	36.5	36.5	35.5	37	36.5	39	41	36.5	36.5	35	35	37.5	36	37	39	38	36	37.5	41	38.5	38
8	40	38.5	37	38	37.5	35.5	37	37.5	39	41.5	36	37	35.5	35	38	36.5	36	38	37.5	36	37.5	40	38.5	37
9	40.5	38	36	36.5	37.5	37.5	35	36	39	41	36	37	35.5	34.5	36	34.5	36	38	37.5	37.5	40	37.5	37.5	36.5
10	39.5	38	35	37.5	36	36	36	35	37	40.5	37	36.5	35.5	35	37	36.5	36.5	38.5	37	37.5	37	40	37.5	37
$\bar{X}$	40	38	36.5	37	36.5	36.5	36	36	38.5	41	36.5	36.5	35.5	34.5	37	35.5	36	38.5	38	36.5	37	40	38	37
R	1	2	4	4.5	3	5	2	2	2.5	1	4.5	1	1	0.5	4.0	2	3.5	1.5	2.5	2	1.5	1	2	1.5

including line operators, in less than ten mintues! There are four simple rules to follow.

Rule 1: Divide the specification width by 4. The boundaries of the middle half of the specification then become the pre-control (P-C) lines. The area between these precontrol lines is called the green zone. The two areas between each precontrol line and each specification limit are called the yellow zones. The two areas beyond the specification limits are called the red zones.

Rule 2: To determine process capability, take a sample of five consecutive units from the process. If all five fall within the green zone, the process is in control. (In fact, with this simple rule, the usual samples of fifty to one hundred units to calculate C_p and C_{pk} are not necessary. By applying the multiplication theorem of probabilities or the binomial distribution, it can be proven that a minimum C_{pk} of 1.33 will automatically result.) Full production can now commence. If even one of the units falls outside the green zone, the process is not in control. Conduct an investigation, using engineering judgment (which is not infallible—by a long shot) or, better still, the design of experiments (detailed in Chapter 5) to determine and reduce the cause of variation.

Rule 3: Once production starts, take two consecutive units from the process periodically. The following possibilities can occur:

A. If both units fall in the green zone, continue production.

B. If one unit is in the green zone and the other in one of the yellow zones, the process is still in control. Continue production.

C. If both units fall in the yellow zones (with both in the same yellow zone or one in one yellow zone and the second in the other), stop production and conduct an investigation into the cause of varia-tion.

D. If even one unit falls in the red zone, there is a known reject, and production must be stopped and the reject cause investigated. When the process is stopped—as in C and D—and the cause of variation identified and reduced (or eliminated), Rule 2—i.e., five units in a row in the green zone—must be reapplied before production can resume.

Rule 4: The frequency of sampling of two consecutive units is determined by dividing the time period between two stoppages (i.e., between two pairs of yellows) by six.* In other words, if there is a stoppage (two yellows), say, at 9 a.m. and the process is corrected and restarted soon after, followed by another stoppage at 12 noon (two yellows again), the period of three hours between these stoppages is divided by six, to give a frequency of sampling of every half hour. If, on the other hand, the period between two stoppages is three days, the frequency of sampling is every half-day.

Figure 6 is a graphical portrayal of precontrol, with a summary of the four simple rules. (The frequency distribution on the right is a special case, where the process width and the specification width are equal. It is only shown as an illustration.)

THE STATISTICAL POWER OF PRECONTROL

The theory behind the effectiveness of precontrol is based on the multiplication theorem of probabilities and the binomial distribution. Although the mathematical derivation of the α and β risks for precontrol is beyond the scope of this briefing, the following is a summary:

- The worst α risk—the risk of overcorrection, i.e., stopping a process when it should continue—is around 2%.
- The worst β risk—the risk of allowing a process to continue when it should be stopped—is close to 1.5%.

*When precontrol was first developed, the time period between two stoppages had to be divided by 24 to determine the frequency of sampling. This was later found to be much too conservative and the number was changed to 6. However, if much greater protection against continuing a process that should be stopped is desired, the frequency of sampling can be increased to 10,12,15—even up to 24. In most industrial applications, however, such an increase is not at all necessary.

Figure 6. Simple precontrol rules.

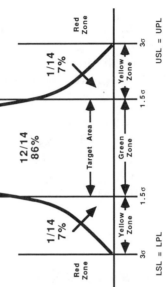

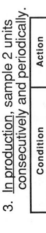

Simple Pre-control Rules:

1. Draw 2 Pre-control (P-C) lines in the middle half of Spec. Width.

2. To determine Process Capability. 5 units in a row must be within P-C lines (green zone).
   If not, use diagnostic tools to reduce variation.

3. In production, sample 2 units consecutively and periodically.

Condition	Action
1. 2 units in Green Zone	Continue
2. 1 unit in Green and 1 unit in Yellow	Continue
3. 2 units in Yellow	Stop*
4. 1 unit in Red	Stop*

* To resume production, 5 units in a row must be within the green zone.

4. Frequency of Sampling.
   Divide the time interval between 2 stoppages by 6.

- When the process width is greater than the specification width—generally C_{pk}s of 0.8 or less—precontrol is so sensitive that it will stop the process at least 99 times out of 100 and force an improvement investigation.
- When the process width is 75% or less of the specification width —C_{pk}s of 1.33 or more—the use of precontrol becomes most productive. The process is in control and precontrol will keep it there.
- When the process width is 50% of the specification width—C_{pk} of 2.0—precontrol will allow hundreds and thousands of units to be produced without a single reject.

The beauty of precontrol, therefore, is that it is an ideal incentive/ penalty tool. It penalizes poor quality by shutting down the process so often that problem solving with the use of design of experiments becomes imperative. It rewards good quality by sampling more and more infrequently. Control charts, on the other hand, have no sampling rule or built-in flexibility to deal with this important feature.

CHARTING PRECONTROL: EASING THE OPERATOR'S BURDEN

As opposed to control charts, a graphical record with a chart is not mandatory in precontrol. The machine or process operator has the simplest of rules—"two greens or one green and one yellow: continue; two yellows or one red: stop." There is no need to distract the operator with long and painful data entries. However, if a precontrol chart is required for historic purposes or as proof of control to a customer, the operator can just make easy slash-mark entries in prerecorded forms with green, yellow, and red zones. Figure 7 is an example of a precontrol chart used to control the thickness of chrome, nickel, and gold deposits on glass in a sputtering machine. In this particular case, the actual readings are also recorded for each precontrol sample of two units. From these readings, C_p and C_{pk} values are easily calculated and histograms plotted, if required. There is no need for manual calculations, hand-held calculators, or expensive computer programs—an important advantage for small suppliers who do not want or need money thrown at a process with expensive control charts.

Figure 7. Typical precontrol chart.

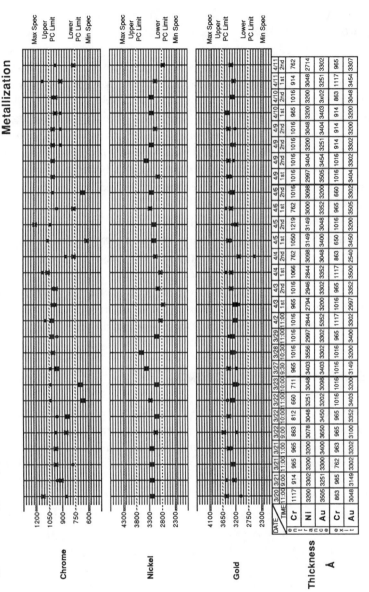

Metallization

	DATE	3/20	3/21	3/21	3/22	3/22	3/22	3/23	3/23	3/27	3/28	3/29	4/2	4/3	4/3	4/4	4/4	4/5	4/5	4/6	4/6	4/9	4/9	4/9	4/9	4/10	4/10	4/11	4/11
	TIME	11:00	9:00	11:00	1:00	9:00	10:00	11:00	10:00	9:30	10:30	11:00	11:00	1st	2nd	1st	2nd	1st	2nd	1st	2nd	1st	2nd	1st	2nd	1st	2nd	1st	2nd
e c i r a c e	Cr	1117	914	965	863	812	660	711	965	1016	1016	1016	1016	965	1016	1066	762	1050	1219	762	1016	1016	1016	1016	1016	965	1016	914	762
	Ni	3200	3302	3200	3078	3048	3251	3048	3403	3556	2997	2844	2946	2794	2844	3098	3000	3149	3149	3098	3404	2997	3505	3200	3200	3048	2714
	Au	3505	3251	3300	3650	3450	3202	3098	3403	3302	5352	3302	3200	3352	3048	3352	3400	3400	3352	3454	3251	3404	3403	3x02	3251	3302
e x i t	Cr	863	965	762	963	965	1016	1016	1016	1016	965	1117	1016	965	965	1117	863	650	1016	660	965	1016	914	1016	914	863	1117	965
	Au	3048	3149	3302	3100	3352	3403	3200	3149	3200	3400	3302	3302	2997	3352	3500	2540	3450	3200	3505	3302	3404	3302	3200	3200	3048	3454	3307

Thickness
Å

TACKLING MULTIPLE QUALITY CHARACTERISTICS

Precontrol is also a far more economical tool in controlling multiple quality characteristics on a product or process. As an example, if the variations in a 36-cavity mold must be monitored in an injection molding machine, the number of readings required to establish even trial control limits in a control chart would average 3,600. By contrast, precontrol would determine process capability with five readings for each cavity, or a total of 180 readings. In monitoring the process, precontrol would require only 40% or 50% of the ongoing readings in control charts. Further, if the process is stable, the sampling rule in precontrol of six samplings between two pairs of yellow would allow those percentages to be reduced to 1 to 10% of control chart samples.

It must also be pointed out that it is not necessary to monitor all parameters of a product or process continuously after initial process capability is confirmed on each parameter. Only the most important or the most troublesome parameters need to be sampled. As an example, in the case of the 36-cavity mold, there may be only three or four cavities with large variations that need ongoing surveillance. The rest can be monitored infrequently or not at all.

THE VERSATILITY OF PRECONTROL

The rule of six samplings between two stoppages need not be associated with time alone. In a very fast operation, where several hundred units are produced in a minute, the quantity of units between two stoppages (two pairs of yellows) can be divided by six to determine sampling frequency.

Precontrol is also a versatile technique in determining when to adjust a process or change a tool, rather than a technique tied to fixed or arbitrary time periods. The time to change is when the process drifts into one or the other yellow region. Two yellows give the signal. It is as simple as that.

Another feature of precontrol is its applicability to one-sided specification limits. As an example, consider a product with a minimum requirement of 10 volts, but no maximum. Instead of two precontrol lines drawn in the middle half of the distance between the lower and upper specification limit, there would now be only a single precontrol line. It would be located midway between a desired target or design center and the lower specification limit. Alternately, it could be located between the product average and the lower specification limit. In the above example, if the design center was at 15 volts, the single precontrol line would be drawn at 12.5 volts. If the average of the product was 16 and the alternative method used, the single precontrol line would be at 13.

CONVERTING ATTRIBUTES INTO VARIABLES: THE "BO DEREK" SCALE

Because precontrol deals primarily with the measurement of continuous values, called variables, it may appear to the uninitiated that it cannot be applied to attributes that deal in discrete numbers, such as accept or reject, pass or fail. They may argue that, whereas precontrol is a better substitute for $\overline{X}$ and R control charts, the use of p and c control charts* is unavoidable. Attributes, however, need not be any limitation whatsoever to precontrol.

The trick is to convert an attribute into an "artificial" variable, using a numerical scale from 1 to 10. In what is humorously called the "Bo Derek" scale, from the actress's movie *Ten*, the number 10 would correspond to perfection in the quality characteristic being measured and the number 1 would equate with the worst possible reject. There would be other grades of quality ranging between these two extremes. As an example, to convert attributes such as paint, color, scratches, gouges, dents, pinholes, etc., into variables, a committee consisting of the customer, sales, engineering, manufacturing, and quality would grade ten physical samples, ranging from a totally unacceptable 1 to a perfect 10. These physical samples would, then, constitute a "variables scale" to determine the appropriate number for a similar defect in production. In case physical samples are too difficult or too inflexible to develop and maintain, color photographs can be substituted. (It may not be necessary to use a full 1

---

*p and c charts suffer from the same fundamental weaknesses as $\overline{X}$ and R charts, and because they deal with attributes they lack the discriminatory power of variables. They are even worse than $\overline{X}$ and R charts and for this reason they will not be discussed in this briefing.

to 10 scale; a truncated 1 to 5 scale can sometimes suffice.) In a numerical scale of this kind, let us assume that the specification limits are from 4 (worst acceptable) to 10 (perfect). Since this is, in reality, a one-sided specification, a single precontrol line would be drawn at 7.

WEIGHTING ATTRIBUTES IN TERMS OF IMPORTANCE

Another weakness of p and c control charts is the practice of lumping all types of defects into a single total for attributes. Such charts lack the sensitivity associated with grading defects by importance. In precontrol, every defect mode is assigned a weight in proportion to its importance. This weight, multiplied by the number of defects in that mode, gives the score for each defect type. These scores, when added up, result in a weighted total for a particular time, and a precontrol chart can then be plotted. Such charts have the effect of a magnified scale and are far more sensitive and pinpointed in terms of defect modes than a catchall p or c chart.

Figure 8 is an example of such a precontrol chart. It expands solder defects, each with its own weight based on the importance of the defect in terms of potential field failure. The precontrol chart highlights the various types of defects found at a particular time; trends with time; and whether or not the weighted defect scores exceed the tight precontrol lines of 50 defects per million connections (i.e., 50 ppm.).

A CAPSULE COMPARISON OF CONTROL CHARTS VS. PRECONTROL

Table 5 is a comparison of control charts and precontrol. It clearly shows the weaknesses of control charts versus the strengths of precontrol in terms of simplicity; use by operators; mathematical complexity; applicability to small production runs; recalibration of control limits; machine adjustments; frequency of sampling; discriminatory power; conversion of attribute charts; and—most important of all—economy.

As a postscript, if precontrol, rather than control charts, had been used in Table 4 to control bushing wear, the very first sample at 8 a.m.

Figure 8. A precontrol chart converting attributes into variables on an expanded scale.

Wave Solder Operation

Code	Pts										
S.S.	+20										XX
N.S.	+10										
Excess	+5										
Capping	+5										
Total											

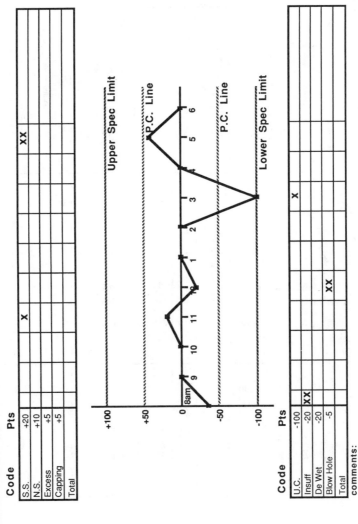

Code	Pts										
U.C.	-100										X
Insuff	-20	XX									
De Wet	-20										
Blow Hole	-5					XX					
Total											

comments:

Table 5. The advantages of precontrol over control charts.

Characteristic	Control Charts	Pre-control
1. Simplicity	• Complex - calculations of control	• Simple - pre-control is middle half of spec. width
2. Use by operators	• Difficult - charting mandatory, interpretation unclear.	• Easy - green and yellow zones, a practical approach for all workers.
3. Mathematical	• Involved - $\bar{X}$, R, control limits and process limits must be calculated.	• Elementary - must only know how to divide by 4.
4. Small production runs	• Useless for production runs below 500 units - sampling of 80 - 150 units before even trial limits can be established.	• Can be used for production runs above 20 units; pre-control lines pre-determined by specs. (which can be narrowed).
5. Re-calibration of control limits	• Frequent - no such thing in industry as a constant cause system.	• None needed, unless specs "goal posts" are moved inward.
6. Machine adjustments	• Time consuming - any adjustment requires another trial run of 80 - 150 units.	• Instant based on 2 units.
7. Frequency of sampling	• Vague, arbitrary	• Simple rule: 6 samplings between 2 stoppages/adjustments
8. Discriminating power	• Weak - α risk of rejection by chart when there are no rejects is high. β risk of acceptance by chart (in control), when there are rejects is high. Little relationship to specs.	• Excellent - α risk of rejection by pre-control is low; < 2% under worst conditions; with C_{pk} of 1.66. β risk <1.36% under worst conditions 0% with C_{pk} of 1.66.
9. Attribute charts	P, C charts do not distinguish between defect mode types or importance.	Attribute charts can be converted to pre-control charts by weighting defect modes and an arbitrary rating scale.
10. Economy	Expensive - calculations, paperwork, larger samples, more frequent sampling long trial runs.	Inexpensive - calculations simple, min. paperwork, small samples, infrequent sampling if quality is good, process capability determined by just 5 units.

would have indicated that the five units checked would have fallen beyond the precontrol lines of 5.001 and 4.999, thus saving one whole day of useless trial runs with control charts!

PRACTICE EXERCISE ON PRECONTROL: THE WIRE BONDER

An automatic wire bonder, which bonds a wire—the thickness of a human hair—to the die and post of a transistor is put on precontrol to maintain statistical control. The integrity of the wire bond is checked with a destructive pull test on the wire. The specification for the bond strength, before the bond is lifted on either side, is a minimum of 6 gm. and a maximum of 14 gm. The initial sample of five units had the following readings: 8.7 gm., 9.0 gm., 9.4 gm., 8.9 gm., 10 gm.

Question 1. What are the values for the precontrol lines?

Question 2. On the basis of the initial sample of five units, is the process in control?

Question 3. How frequently should a sample of two units be tested for bond strength, assuming that when full production began the period between stoppages (two pairs of yellow) averaged twelve hours?

Question 4. During subsequent production, the results of two sample units, drawn periodically from the process, were as follows:

Sample No.	Unit 1	Unit 2	Action
1	9.4	9.0	————
2	9.0	8.8	————
3	8.9	8.6	————
4	8.5	8.1	————
5	8.4	8.0	————
6	8.0	8.0	————
7	8.0	7.6	————
8	7.5	7.3	————
9	13.0	13.0	————
10	12.0	12.0	————
11	11.6	11.4	————
12	11.0	10.8	————

What action would you take on each sample: Would you continue production or stop?

Question 5. What nonrandom trends do you detect in the data in Question 4? Explain your answer.

Question 6. Assuming that there was no upper specification limit of 14 gm., where would you draw a single precontrol line if the target (or desired) bond strength was at 11.0 gm.?

Here are the answers to our six questions.

Question 1. Precontrol lines are at 8 and 12 gm.

Question 2. Process in control. All five units in the initial sample are within the precontrol lines (green zones).

Question 3. Sampling frequency should be 12 hours/6 = 2 hours.

Question 4. Action on sample numbers 1 through 7 and 10 through 12: Continue production. Action on sample numbers 8 and 9: Stop production. (In actual practice, the process must be adjusted or corrected after sample number 8 and then five more units drawn and determined to be within the green zone before the sampling of two units is resumed. The same holds for sample number 9.)

Question 5. There are three nonrandom trends in the data associated with question 4: (1) Bond strengths are getting lower and lower until a correction is made after sample number 8. Probable cause is bond contamination or loss of bond energy. In any case, the trend needs to be investigated, quite apart from whether production continues or stops. (2) The second reading in each sample is almost always lower than the first. The probable cause may be in the measuring instrument or in the fixture. (3) Sample number 9 indicates an overcorrection (pull strengths too high).

Question 6. With the target at 11.0 gm. and only a single (lower) specification limit, the precontrol line should be midway between the target of 11.0 gm. and the lower specification limit of 6.0 gm., i.e., at 8.5 gm.

Chapter 3

The Measurement of Process Capability

In cycle time management, it is often said that inventory is evil; that inventory is the graveyard of poor management. Similarly, in quality control, variation is evil and large variation is the graveyard of poor quality management. Why is this so? Why has the brand-new discipline of variation reduction become—in a few short years—one of the most important tasks of the development engineer, manufacturing engineer, and quality professional?

CUSTOMERS WANT PRODUCT UNIFORMITY: "LIKE PEAS IN A POD"

There are two reasons. First is the economic loss occasioned by customer dissatisfaction. In the United States, it is widely assumed that if a product parameter is brought within specifications, the customer will be quite happy. Figure 9a portrays this U.S. view—that no matter how narrowly a parameter falls within a specification limit, the customer will be 100% satisfied, and that no matter how narrowly a parameter falls outside a specification limit, the customer will be 100% dissatisfied. In actual practice, there is nothing so digital

Figure 9. The need for variation reduction.

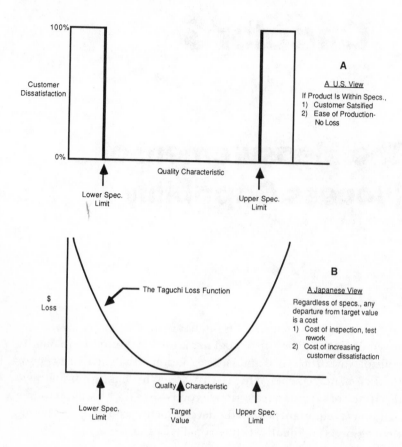

about customer satisfaction (assuming, to begin with, that the specification limits are right). Figure 9b portrays a more realistic Japanese view—that customer dissatisfaction is at zero when a product parameter is at, or very close to, a target value or desired design center, and that it increases exponentially as the parameter moves away from the target value toward one end or the other of the specification limit. Loss of customer satisfaction can be measured in monetary terms. In fact, Genichi Taguchi of Japan has developed a loss function—a quadratic equation—to approximate this loss. Customers want uniformity of product, consistency—not units that vary all over the map, even if they fall within specification. This consistency is a feature of Japanese products that is seldom recognized by American manufacturers.

SCRAP, REPAIR, INSPECTION AND TEST ADD NO VALUE

A second reason why variation is evil is that it perpetuates and institutionalizes the deplorable practice of scrap and repair, analyzing and rework, which is required to get a unit within its specification limits. *The only sure-fire method to eliminate this waste is to so design a product and its process that the parameter is brought close to the target value or design center.* There is no other way to get 100% yields the first time round or to achieve zero defects. Once this is done, production becomes a breeze, and manufacturing can then throw things together without the necessity of inspection and test, which add no value whatsoever.

INTRODUCTION TO PROCESS CAPABABILITY: Cp

Before the variation in a parameter can be reduced, however, it must be measured. Two yardsticks, C_p and C_{pk}, have become standard terminologies in recent years. Process capability, Cp, is approximately defined as specification width (S) divided by process width (P). It is a measure of spread. Figure 10 depicts six frequency distributions comparing the specification width (always 40 - 20 = 20) to the process width.

1. Process A in Figure 10 has a process width of 30 (as defined by traditional $\pm 3\sigma$ limits) to give a C_p of 0.67. It is a process that is out of control, with 2½% reject tails at both ends. This used to be the norm for U.S. processes before the S.P.C. age of the 1980s. Today, there are at least 30% of U.S. processes that are at or below this stage. They compensate for such an out-of-control condition by brute-force sorting, scrap, and rework.

2. Process B has the process width equal to the specification width to give a C_p of 1.0. Although somewhat better than process A, it too can be considered almost out of control because any slight change or drift will cause rejects. At least 60% of U.S. processes have not

Figure 10. C_p—a measure of variation.

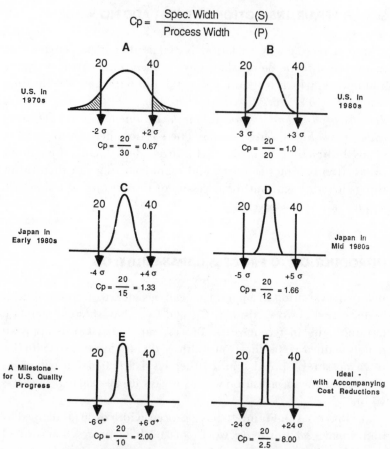

(Upper Spec. Limit = 40; Lower Spec. Limit = 20;
Process Width Defined As ± 3 Sigma Limits)

$$C_p = \frac{\text{Spec. Width} \quad (S)}{\text{Process Width} \quad (P)}$$

A

20   40

U.S. In
1970s

-2 σ   +2 σ

$C_p = \dfrac{20}{30} = 0.67$

B

20   40

U.S. In
1980s

-3 σ   +3 σ

$C_p = \dfrac{20}{20} = 1.0$

C

20   40

Japan In
Early 1980s

-4 σ   +4 σ

$C_p = \dfrac{20}{15} = 1.33$

D

20   40

Japan In
Mid 1980s

-5 σ   +5 σ

$C_p = \dfrac{20}{12} = 1.66$

E

20   40

A Milestone -
for U.S. Quality
Progress

-6 σ*   +6 σ*

$C_p = \dfrac{20}{10} = 2.00$

F

20   40

Ideal -
with Accompanying
Cost Reductions

-24 σ   +24 σ

$C_p = \dfrac{20}{2.5} = 8.00$

* An Alternative Way To Describe Variation Is In Terms Of Standard Deviation - Sigma (σ). In Process B, The Spec. Limits Are At ±3 σ. In Process E, The Spec. Limits Are At ± 6 σ — Virtually A 100% Yield Process.

advanced beyond a C_p of 1.0. So much for our much vaunted S.P.C.!

3. Process C has a C_p of 1.33, showing a margin of safety between the tighter process limits and the specification limits. The Japanese used a C_p of 1.33 as a standard for their important parameters in the early 1980s.

4. Process D, with a C_p of 1.66 is better, with an even wider safety margin.

5. Process E, with a C_p of 2.0, is an important milestone in the march toward variation reduction. Here the process width is only half the specification width. Some of the more progressive companies in the United States, including the author's, have established a C_p of 2.0 as a minimum standard for their own as well as for their suppliers' important quality characteristics.

6. Process F, with a C_p of 8.0, is not only much better; it is also attainable and at a lower overall cost!

In fact, there is no limit to higher and higher C_ps, of 10, 15 and more, so long as no recurring costs are added to the product or process and only the cost of design of experiments, discussed in Chapter 5, is incurred. These experimental costs should be looked upon as an investment rather than as a cost, in the best tradition of quality cost prevention. *It has been this author's experience that not only are costs not added with higher C_ps, they are actually reduced; and that the time it takes to go from C_ps of 1.0 or less to C_ps of 5.0 and more is not measured in years but in weeks—generally with no more than one, two, or three well-designed experiments!*

C_{p_k}—A BETTER MEASURE OF VARIATION AND PROCESS CAPABILITY

C_p is used only as a simple introduction to the concept of process capability. It does not take into account any noncentering of the process relative to the specification limits of a parameter. Such noncentering reduces the margin of safety and, therefore, has a penalty imposed, called a "K" or correction factor. The formulas are:

$$C_p = S/P$$

$$K = \frac{D\text{-}\overline{X}}{S/2} \text{ or } \frac{\overline{X}\text{-}D}{S/2} \text{ (whichever makes K positive)}$$

$$C_{p_k} = (1\text{-}K)\,C_p$$

where:

S = specification width; P = process width ($\pm 3\,\sigma$ limits); D = design center (D need not be at the midpoint of the specification width); $\overline{X}$ = process average.

Figure 11. C_{p_k}—a measure of process capability.

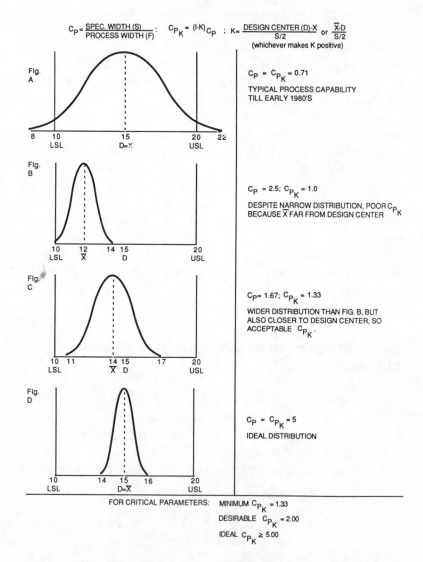

$C_P = \dfrac{\text{SPEC. WIDTH (S)}}{\text{PROCESS WIDTH (F)}}$; $C_{P_K} = (1-K)C_P$; $K = \dfrac{\text{DESIGN CENTER (D)-X}}{S/2}$ or $\dfrac{\overline{X}-D}{S/2}$
(whichever makes K positive)

Fig. A

$C_P = C_{P_K} = 0.71$

TYPICAL PROCESS CAPABILITY
TILL EARLY 1980'S

8   10   15   20   22
     LSL   D=X   USL

Fig. B

$C_P = 2.5$; $C_{P_K} = 1.0$

DESPITE NARROW DISTRIBUTION, POOR C_{P_K}
BECAUSE $\overline{X}$ FAR FROM DESIGN CENTER

10 12 14 15   20
LSL X   D   USL

Fig. C

$C_P = 1.67$; $C_{P_K} = 1.33$

WIDER DISTRIBUTION THAN FIG. B, BUT
ALSO CLOSER TO DESIGN CENTER, SO
ACCEPTABLE C_{P_K}.

10 11   14 15   17   20
LSL   X D   USL

Fig. D

$C_P = C_{P_K} = 5$

IDEAL DISTRIBUTION

10   14 15 16   20
LSL   D=X   USL

FOR CRITICAL PARAMETERS: MINIMUM $C_{P_K} = 1.33$
DESIRABLE $C_{P_K} = 2.00$
IDEAL $C_{P_K} \geq 5.00$

When the process average, $\overline{X}$, and the design center, D, or target value, coincide, K is reduced to zero, making C_p and C_{p_k} equal. If, however, the process average is skewed toward one end or the other of a specification limit, away from the design center, D, the value of K increases, causing a decrease in C_{p_k}, relative to C_p.

This is illustrated in Figure 11. Figure A has a wide spread, with a C_p of 0.71. Since its design center, D, and its average, $\overline{X}$, coincide, the C_p and C_{pk} values are the same at 0.71. Figure B has a narrow spread, with a respectable C_p of 2.5. But because it is located close to the lower specification limit, the K factor penalizes it to give a poor C_{pk} of 1.0. Figure C has a broader spread than Figure B, with a lower C_p of 1.67. But it is closer to the design center, D, than is Figure B and so the K factor has less of a penalty, resulting in a C_{pk} of 1.33—better than Figure B. Figure D is ideal, with both a very narrow spread and a centered process, to give a C_p and C_{pk} of 5.0

C_{pk} is an excellent measure of variability and process capability because it takes into account both spread and noncentering. (In process control, centering a process is much easier than reducing spread. Centering requires only a simple adjustment, whereas spread reduction often requires the patient application of design of experiment techniques.) As in C_p, the objective should be to attain a higher and higher C_{pk}, with a C_{pk} of 2.0 considered merely as a passing milestone on the march past zero defects to near-zero variation. C_{pk} is also a convenient and effective method of specifying supplier quality, better than the old 1% and 2% acceptable quality levels (AQLs) or even the newer and lower defect levels expressed in parts per million (ppm.)

PRACTICE EXERCISE ON C_p AND C_{pk}: THE PRESS BRAKE

A press brake is set up to produce a formed part to a dimension of $3 \pm 0.005''$. A process capability study reveals that the process limits are at $3.002 \pm 0.006''$, ie., at a minimum of 2.996'' and a maximum of 3.008''. After corrective action, the process limits are brought under control to $3.001 \pm 0.002''$.

Question 1: Calculate the C_p and C_{pk} of the old process.

Question 2: Calculate the C_p and C_{pk} of the corrected process.

These are the answers to the practice exercise on C_p and C_{pk}:

Question 1: Specification width (S) = 0.010''; Process width (P) = 0.012''

So, C_p = S/P = 0.010/0.012 = 0.833

$\overline{X}$ = 3.002''; Design Center(D) = 3.000''

So, $K = \dfrac{\overline{X} - D}{S/2} = \dfrac{3.002 - 3.000}{0.005} = \dfrac{0.002}{0.005} = 0.4$

Therefore $C_{pk} = (1 - K)C_p = (1 - 0.4)\,0.833 = 0.5$

Question 2: Specification width (S) = 0.010″; Process width (P) = 0.004″

So, $C_p = S/P = 0.010/0.004 = 2.5$

$\overline{X} = 3.001″$; Design Center(D) = 3.000″

So, $K = \dfrac{\overline{X} - D}{S/2} = \dfrac{3.001 - 3.000}{0.005} = \dfrac{0.001}{0.005} = 0.2$

Therefore $C_{pk} = (1 - K)C_p = (1 - 0.2)\,2.5 = 2.0$

Chapter 4

Variation—An Industrial Epidemic

MEASUREMENT DOES NOT EQUATE WITH IMPROVEMENT

Chapter 3 quantified variation with the introduction of C_p and C_{pk}. But measuring variation does nothing to reduce it. An analogy from the world of dieting is à propros. Thousands get up on their weighing scales each day to wage the battle of the bulge. If measurement alone could do the trick, Americans would be the thinnest people on earth! What is needed is an honest analysis of the causes of overweight— eating habits, type of food, lack of exercise, etc.—before a disciplined regimen of weight reduction is begun. Similarly, the many causes of variation in industry should be analyzed before a systematic attack on variation is mounted. Variation is so widespread in industry that it can be likened to an epidemic. *The new quality mission, therefore, is to inoculate products and processes against variation.*

THE MANY SOURCES OF VARIATION

This chapter will outline the many sources of variation, their underlying causes, and the general approaches to variation reduction. Table 6 presents a capsule summary. The major sources of variation

Table 6. Sources, causes and reduction of variation.

Source	Causes of Variation	Variation Reduction
Poor Management	• No knowledge of or policy on variation reduction • No resources or time allocated to D.O.E. • No championship or involvement in D.O.E. • No D.O.E. training or its implementation • S.P.C. and control charts-especially for problem solving.	• Top management training in D.O.E. overview • Management steering committee for D.O.E. • D.O.E. training and workshops for tech. population • Monitoring the D.O.E "Process" rather than just goals and results
Poor Product/ Process Specs.	• Selling over marketing • Pushing state of art designs • Wide tolerances vs. target values • Reliability not a specification • No D.O.E. in systems testing	• Value research and multi-attribute competitive analysis tools • Evolutionary vs. revolution designs • Target values and use of loss funtion • Optimizing old equipment, not junking it. • Multiple environment overstress tests for reliability • Extension of D.O.E. in customer application
Poor Component Specs.	• Fascination with technology • Indiscriminate and tight tolerances • Boiler plate specs; supplier published specs. • Monte Carlo and worst case analysis • Formulas linking variables non-existent, wrong or unable to determine interaction effects.	• D.O.E. techniques at pilot run stage to separate important variables from unimportant ones. (Part B for detailed techniques)
Inadequate Quality System	• Comprehensive quality system not developed. • Quality peripherals overlooked.	• Infrastrucure of a quality system • Postrol; process certification; pre control
Poor Supplier Materials	• Too many suppliers • Control by negotiations and tablepounding • AQL, Incoming Inspection	• "Best in class" Partnership supplier • Physical proximity, continous help • D.O.E. training • C_{P_K} of 2.0 as a minimum
"Operator" Errors	• Poor instructions, training • Poor processes, materials, equipment • Design for non-manufacturability • External inspection • "Pair of hands" syndrome	• Training in 7 Q.C. tools and D.O.E. • Encourgement, support, management involvement • Self inspection and poka yoke (fool proofing) • Gain sharing

can be grouped into six categories: (1) poor management; (2) poor product/process specifications; (3) poor component specifications; (4) inadequate quality system; (5) poor supplier materials; and (6) "operator" errors.

POOR MANAGEMENT

Deming and Juran assert that 85% of quality problems are caused by management, and only 15% by workers on the line. They are being kind to management: the split is actually closer to 95-5. Although there are many dimensions to the quality problems caused by management, its sins of omission and commission with respect to variation include the following:

- Lack of knowledge about the impact of variation on overall quality and cost.
- No coherent policy on variation reduction.
- No resources or time allocated to the design of experiments (D.O.E), but unlimited quantities of both expended on fire fighting.
- No leadership in variation reduction in terms of goals, sponsorship, championship, or involvement.
- No D.O.E training or no follow-up of training with implementation.
- Equating quality progress with S.P.C. and control charts.

How very different from an enlightened management philosophy, as illustrated by a directive from William Scollard, Vice-President of Engineering and Manufacturing at Ford: "Our new quality thinking should be reduced process variability around the nominal as an operating philosophy for never-ending quality improvement."

The attack on variability in management must begin with an understanding of the economics of variation reduction. It requires a top management steering committee to launch training in D.O.E., followed by workshops and learning by doing for the technical people. The committee should also be involved in the D.O.E. "process" for improvement, not just limit itself to formulating high-sounding goals and tracking results in sterile operation reviews.

POOR PRODUCT/PROCESS SPECIFICATIONS

Most product specifications are either vague, arbitrary, or wrong. Process specifications are even worse! A major cause of this variation lies in the difference between selling and marketing. In selling, management or the engineer determines product requirements in isolation and then forces the product down the throats of customers, through slick advertising and other high-pressure tactics. In marketing, the company first makes a painstaking effort to explore what the customer wants and then designs products to fit those needs. It is tragic that eighty years after Julius Rosenwald and Robert Wood laid the foundations of marketing and with it built Sears Roebuck into a giant merchandiser, most American companies still "sell" rather than "market" their products. The worst crime in this source of variations is to design and build products efficiently—even with zero defects—that the customer does not want!

There are proven techniques by which to translate the "voice of the customer" into meaningful product specifications. Ten years ago the Japanese launched a new discipline called quality function deployment (Q.F.D.). It is needlessly complex, however, and unsuited to the American temperament. Fortunately, there are simpler techniques developed in the United States, such as value research, multi-attribute competitive analysis, and PIMs (Profit Impact of Market Strategy) analysis of customer perceptions, that are more effective and less costly than Q.F.D. Lamentably, they are little known and even less used.

Other reasons for poor product/process specifications are:

- The engineer's ego in creating a "state of the art" design, with his name etched onto it in perpetuity.
- Use of broad specification limits and tolerances rather than a focus on target values or design centers for product/process parameters.
- Infrequent use of reliability, in mean-time-between-failures (MTBF), or mean-time-between-assists (MTBA), as a specification.
- Lack of systems testing in the customer's application, with a design of experiments approach to identify important and interacting variables.

The variation reduction antidotes are to:

- Use an evolutionary, rather than a revolutionary, approach to product/process design—one in which no more than a fourth of the design is changed at a given time.
- Establish target values and the (Taguchi) loss function.
- Save and optimize old processes through D.O.E., rather than junk them in favor of capital-intensive new equipment with its own host of problems.
- Utilize multiple environment overstress tests as the most powerful tool in reducing product/process variations in reliability.
- Extend design of experiments to field testing at the customer's site.

POOR COMPONENT SPECIFICATIONS

Even assuming that product specifications have been optimized as shown above, there is another major pitfall—the inadequate conversion of product specifications into component specifications. The reasons are:

- Engineering's fascination with technology.
- Engineering's proclivity toward indiscriminate and tight tolerances.
- Engineering's reliance on previous component drawings, "boiler plate" requirements, or supplier's published specifications.
- Reliance on the computer for determining component tolerances. This can only be done if the formula for governing the relationship between the output (or dependent variable) and the independent component variables is known. In many complex designs, involving scores of independent variables, even an Einstein could not develop such a formula. This is a major weakness in a Monte Carlo simulation exercise.
- A "worst case" analysis and design with an extremely low probability of occurrence in actual practice. This is an appreciable addition to cost with no value added.
- Little or no knowledge of the interaction effects, either second-order or higher-order, between component variables even when there is a mathematical formula for the relationships between variables.

All these excess variations can be overcome—at the prototype, engineering pilot run, or production pilot run stage—by well designed experiments, fully detailed in Part II, that can separate the important variables from the unimportant ones.

INADEQUATE QUALITY SYSTEM

Besides management, product, process, materials, and workmanship, there are many quality peripherals that can cause variation. Poor instructions, lack of environmental controls, lack of preventive maintenance, and test instrument variations are but a few examples. The control of these types of variation requires a comprehensive quality system, along with techniques like positrol and process certification. Chapter 13 is devoted to reining in these quality peripherals.

POOR SUPPLIER MATERIALS*

Next to design, variations in supplier materials contribute the most to poor quality. The traditional approach of having multiple suppliers for the same part to assure quality, delivery, and cost is obsolete and counterproductive. So are negotiations, table pounding, and quality improvement by fiat and by remote control. So are AQL, sampling plans, and incoming inspection. The only way to improve supplier quality and to reduce variability is to:

- Demonstrate, first, that your own company is highly professional in the field of quality in general, and in the design of experiments in particular.
- Ascertain that the supplier is both committed to improvement and capable of entering into a long-term partnership with you.
- Select a supplier who is in physical proximity to you and small enough and hungry enough to accept your professional coaching in D.O.E. techniques.

*A recommended reference text is this author's *Supply Management: How to Make U.S. Suppliers Competitive*, published by the American Management Association. It deals with improving supplier quality, cost, and cycle time, within the framework of a partnership relationship with "best-in-class" suppliers.

- Specify minimum C_{pk}s of 2.0 and more for important parameters, bypassing the useless milestones of AQLs, PPMs, sampling plans, and postmortem incoming inspection.

"OPERATOR" ERRORS

Operator variations and inconsistencies are the causes of quality problems most frequently cited by orthodox management. Such citations, however, almost always reflect a general ignorance of quality—management at its quality worst. Worker defects are only the effects. The underlying causes are more likely to be:

- Poor instructions, goals, training, and supervision
- Poor processes, materials, test equipment
- Poor design for manufacturability
- Use of external inspection as a crutch
- Assumption that workers are but a "pair of hands"—hired from the neck down!

When these roadblocks to quality work are removed, workers— 99% of whom are well-motivated to begin with—will almost always come through with sterling performance. The steps to variation reduction in this area—in general terms—are: encouragement; support; the elimination of fear; and management's mingling among and active involvement with the workers. Financial incentives for improved performance, such as gain-sharing, should also be given serious consideration.

In specific terms, there should be a concerted move away from external inspection to neighbor inspection and, eventually, self-inspection, aided by "poka yoke" (foolproof) methods, such as the use of automatic equipment and sensors to buttress visual checks. More important, workers can not only be trained in the seven tools of Q.C. as practiced widely by Japanese line workers; they can also be trained in the even easier design of experiment tools described in Part II. It has been this author's experience that some of the most adventurous and rewarding D.O.E. work has been conducted by line workers and technicians, once trained, more than by their more cautious and conservative engineering counterparts.

Part II:

The Design of Experiments (D.O.E): Key To the Magic Kingdom of Quality

Chapter 5

Three Approaches to D.O.E.: Classical, Taguchi, and Shainin

Chapter 3 dealt with the measurement of variation, introducing C_p and C_{pk} as parameters. Chapter 4 outlined the many causes of variation and listed general variation reduction techniques. Subsequent chapters will concentrate on the most powerful of these techniques, generically called the design of experiments (D.O.E.). They are particularly important in two areas: for resolving chronic quality problems in production, and at the design stage of both product and process. A chronic problem can be described as a product with an unacceptable defect rate, one that is measurable in higher dollar waste and that has defied traditional engineering solutions for a long time. (Some chronic problems have one, two, and three birthday candles on them!) D.O.E. techniques are especially important on all *new designs,* so that chronic quality problems in production can be *prevented* before fire fighting becomes necessary.

The *objectives* in both areas are to:

- Identify the important variables—whether they be product or process parameters; materials or components from suppliers;

environmental or measuring equipment factors.

- Separate these—generally no more than one to four—important variables.
- Reduce the variation on the important variables (including the tight control of interaction effects) through close tolerancing, redesign, supplier process improvement, etc.
- Open up the tolerances on the unimportant variables to reduce costs substantially.

CLASSICAL VS. TAGUCHI VS. SHAININ D.O.E.

There are three approaches to the design of experiments—the classical, Taguchi, and Shainin. The classical approach is based on the pioneering work of Sir Ronald Fisher, who applied design of experiment techniques to the field of agriculture as early as the 1930s. It is difficult to conceive of an application in which there are as many variables—and as many interacting variables—as agriculture. In the United States, classical D.O.E. has been extended to chemical processes. Beyond these disciplines, it has remained in the province of academia. Its principal champions are Box and Hunter, two eminent professors and statistical authorities.

Dr. Genichi Taguchi of Japan adapted the classical approach to develop the technique of orthogonal arrays. While the Taguchi methods have not been universally accepted in Japan, many leading Japanese companies have adopted them. One of these—Nippon Denso—conducts 2,500 Taguchi experiments each year, probably more than the total of D.O.E. experiments of all kinds in the entire United States! In this country, AT&T and Ford have promoted Taguchi methods. As a result, several companies such as Xerox, I.T.T., United Technologies, and some Ford suppliers have started to use the orthogonal array approach, with marginal success.

The third D.O.E. approach is a collection of techniques taught by Dorian Shainin, a consultant to more than six hundred leading companies in the United States. Unfortunately for this country, Shainin's methods have not received the publicity they so richly deserve.

Table 7, under techniques, lists the principal methods used by each approach. The classical tools start with fraction factorials and end with evolutionary optimization (EVOP). The Taguchi methods

Table 7. Three approaches to the design of experiments.

Characteristic	Classical	Taguchi	Shainin
Technique	• Fractional Factorials, EVOP, etc.	• Orthogonal arrays	• Multi-vari, variable search, full factorials
Effectiveness	• Moderate (20% to 200% improvement) • Retrogression possible	• Low to moderate (20% to 100% improvement) • Retrogression likely	• Extremely powerful (100% to 500% improvement) • No retrogression
Cost	• Moderate • Average of 50 experiments	• High • Average of 50 to 100 experiments	• Low • Average of 20 experiments
Complexity	• Moderate • Full ANOVA required	• High • Inner and outer array multiplication, S/N, ANOVA	• Low • Experiments can be understood by line operators
Statistical Validity	• Low • Higher order interaction effects confounded with main effects • To a lesser extent, even 2nd order interaction effects confounded	• Poor • No randomization • Even 2nd order interaction effects confounded with main effects • S/N concept good	• High • Every variable tested with all levels of every other variable • Excellent separation and quantification of main and interaction effects
Applicability	• Requires hardware • Main use in production	• Primary use as a substitute for Monte Carlo analysis	• Requires hardware • Can be used as early as prototype and engineering run stage
Ease of Implementation	• Moderate • Engineering and statistical knowledge required	• Difficult • Engineers not likely to use technique	• Easy • Even line workers can conduct experiments

use orthogonal arrays (inner and outer) in "tolerance design," employing analysis of variance and signal-to-noise for statistical evaluation. Each of the Shainin methods is detailed, chapter by chapter.

All three approaches are far superior to conventional S.P.C., which attempts to solve chronic problems by means of control charts—a total waste of time. All three approaches are also far superior to old-fashioned experiments, taught in universities and widely practiced by traditional engineers, in which one variable at a time is varied, with all other variables kept rigidly constant. Besides the inordinate amount of time needed for such experimentation, the central statistical weakness of this approach is the chronic inability to separate main from interaction effects. The results are frustration, the endless chasing of one's own tail, and high costs.

THE TROUBLE WITH TAGUCHI

The greatest blessing that Taguchi has conferred on industry is that he has taken design of experiments out of the rarefied realm of university professors and statisticians and into the design laboratories and production floors of industry. His methods can be summed up in the motto: "Don't just sit there, do something!"

Nevertheless, his orthogonal arrays approach has several fundamental flaws. To start with, it is complicated. Engineers are uncomfortable with even simple statistical concepts, such as standard deviation, not to mention analysis of variance, F tests, and signal-to-noise ratios. It is also expensive. With inner arrays multiplied by outer arrays, the number of experiments can reach several hundred.

Further, it does not believe in randomization. This is a cardinal statistical sin, because variables not included in the experiments should be allowed equal opportunities of entering or leaving the experiments. The Taguchi approach selects factors to be included in the experiment through brainstorming. This is a highly subjective technique, it introduces too many variables, and wastes time and money. (By contrast, the Shainin approach, of homing in on the family of the important variables, through techniques like the multivari and component search, greatly reduces the number of experiments required.)

It does not consider interactions, unless, on the basis of engineering judgment, a severe interaction is "suspected." This is a grave structural flaw in the Taguchi design. One can seldom guess even the main variables that contribute to variation, let alone interactions between them.

The orthogonal array* belongs in the family of fraction factorials and suffers from the same statistical weaknesses as that generic family of saturated designs, namely the confounding of interaction effects (especially the higher-order interaction effects) with main effects.

In short, its results are suboptimal, with benefits that can and do evaporate.

THE SHAININ DIAGNOSTIC TOOLS

Fortunately for America, Dorian Shainin—along with his pioneering contribution to reliability perfection, through multiple environment overstress tests—has given us D.O.E. tools that can diagnose and greatly reduce variation, leading us beyond zero defects, beyond the milestone of C_{pk} of 2.0, to near-zero variability. These tools are:

- *Simple*—understood by engineers and line workers alike. The mathematics involved are unbelievably—almost embarrassingly—elementary!
- *Logical*—based on common sense.
- *Practical*—easy to implement—in production, in design, with suppliers.
- *Universal in scope*—applicable in a wide range of industries, big and small, process-intensive as well as assembly-intensive.
- *Statistically powerful*—in terms of accuracy, with no violations of statistical principles.
- *Excellent in terms of results*—with quality gains not in the inconsequential range of 10-50% improvement but in the 100-500% range!

*Recently, a published Taguchi case study was used to compare the Taguchi orthogonal array with Shainin's variables search technique (Chapter 5). The data from the case study was replaced with random numbers. This should give results that are insignificant; i.e., no one factor should outrank another. The procedure was followed for three trials. One trial out of three failed the test because one or more factors outranked others. The same random data were then used in variables search. In each case, the results were insignificant, as they should be. In other words, the Taguchi method is not sensitive enough to distinguish between important and unimportant variables under all conditions. This could lead to erroneous decisions about changing a process or product. Variables search, by contrast, is completely rigorous and does have the sensitivity required to distinguish between levels of significance and insignificance.

Figure 12. Variation reduction—a roadmap.

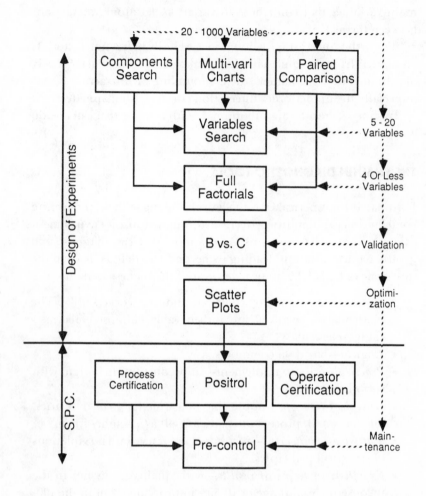

Table 7 compares the classical vs. Taguchi vs. Shainin methods in terms of effectiveness, cost, complexity, statistical validity, applicability, and ease of implementation. It is obvious that the Shainin tools run circles around the other two in almost every characteristic. They can help America leapfrog the Japanese in their own game of concentration on design over production quality.

Table 8. The 7 D.O.E. tools.

Technique	Objective	Where Applicable	When Applicable	Sample Size
Multi-vari Chart	1. Discover family of red X-position, cycle or time patterns 2. Detect non-random patterns	Wherever stratified samples of consecutive units, at different times, can be measured	1. At engineering pilot run; production pilot run; During production-problem-solving 2. During production-problem-solving	≥ 9
Components Search	Home in on a few key variables from a wide variety of variables to capture family of red X or red X itself	Where there are good and bad assemblies, capable of being disassembled and reassembled	1. When only a few units are available (prototype stage or in pilot runs) 2. During production - problem-solving	2
Paired Comparisons	Same as components search	Wherever there are good and bad assemblies or components that cannot be dis-assembled	Mainly in production, field returns or in failure analysis	≥ 12
Variables Search	1. Pinpoint red X, pink X, etc. 2. To separate and quantify the main effects and inter-action effects of variables	Homing in on the culprit variables following multi-vari, components search or paired comparison experiments	1. When more than 4 variables are investigated 2. At prototype, pilot run stages 3. In production problem-solving	• 6 to 16 tests for 5 variables • 2 more tests for each additional variable
Full Factorials	Same as variable search	Same as variables search	1. When 4 or less variables are investigated 2. Same as variables search 3. Same as variables search	• Max. 16 or 32 tests
B vs. C	1. Evaluate a minimum amount of superiority of method B over method C or vice-versa Select B or C if there is no performance difference, but a definite cost difference	1. As a validation of red X, pink X factors selected in variables search or full factorial experiments 2. When problem is easy to solve, use as the only experiment, bypassing other techniques	1. In prototype or pilot run stages 2. In production, as a capping run 3. In nontechnical fields-sales, advertising, human relations etc. - a universal tool	Usually 3 B's and 3 C's
Scatter Plots	1. Determine optimum values of important variables 2. Cost reduction of unimportant variables	Following previous 6 techniques	In pilot run of production stage	30

VARIATION REDUCTION: A DETECTIVE JOURNEY TO THE RED X.

Figure 12 represents a time-tested roadmap to variation reduction. It consists of seven D.O.E. tools invented or perfected by Dorian Shainin. They are based on his philosophy: "Don't let the engineers do the guessing; let the parts do the talking." The analogy of a detective story is appropriate in this diagnostic journey, shown in Figure 12. Clues can be gathered with each D.O.E. tool, each progressively more positive, until the culprit cause—the Red X in the Shainin lexicon—is captured, reduced, and controlled. The second most important cause is called the Pink X, the third most important the Pale Pink X. Generally, by the time the top one, two, or three causes—the Red X, Pink X, and Pale Pink X—are captured, well over 80% of the variation allowed within the specification limits is eliminated. *In short, a minimum C_{pk} of 5.0 is achieved—not in five years, not in four, three, two, or even one year, not even in months— but with just one, two, or three D.O.E. experiments!*

Table 8 presents a capsule summary of each of the seven D.O.E. tools, their objectives, and where and when each is applicable, and gives a sample size, depicting the unbelievable economy of experimentation.

S.P.C. TOOLS: THE TAIL THAT HAS BEEN WAGGING THE D.O.E. DOG

It is only when the diagnostic journey, using the D.O.E. tools depicted in Figure 12, has ended—with a substantial reduction in variation—that we can afford to descend from the highlands of D.O.E. to the lowlands of S.P.C. The true role of S.P.C., therefore, is *maintenance* to assure that variation, once captured and reduced, is incarcerated in a maximum security prison. These S.P.C. tools, shown in Figure 12, will be discussed in detail in Chapter 13 (with the exception of precontrol, already treated in depth in Chapter 2).

Yet if a poll were taken in American industry, among those companies that have attempted variation reduction, 90% would start with S.P.C.—a clear case of the S.P.C. tail wagging the D.O.E. dog. And 90% of *them* would equate S.P.C. with little more than control charts!

Chapter 6

Multi-Vari Charts:
To Home in on the Red X

The main *purpose* of a multi-vari chart is to reduce a large number of possible causes (or factors or variables—these are synonymous terms) of variation to a much smaller family of variables, containing the Red X. This narrows the field of inquiry from, say, 30 to 100 variables or more, down to a more manageable number, for instance 1 to 20. These prime suspects can then be further narrowed down to the Red X and Pink X with a variables search or full factorials. In several cases, the clues from a multi-vari chart are strong enough to directly pinpoint the Red X, precluding the need for further experiments.

MULTI-VARI CHART METHODOLOGY

A multi-vari chart is a stratified experiment to determine whether the major variation pattern is positional, cyclical, or temporal (time-related). If the greatest variation is temporal, the several factors contributing to positional or cyclical variations can be eliminated or given a much lower priority for further investigation. Examples in each pattern of variation are:

(Positional)

- "Variations within a single unit (e.g., porosity in a metal casting) or across a single unit with many parts (e.g., a printed circuit board with many components).
- Variations by location in a batch-loading process (e.g., cavity-to-cavity variations in a mold process).
- Variations from machine-to-machine; operator-to-operator; or plant-to-plant.

(Cyclical)

- Variation between consecutive units drawn from a process.
- Variation among groups of units.
- Batch-to-batch variations.
- Lot-to-lot variations.

(Temporal)

- Variations from hour-to-hour; shift-to-shift; day-to-day; week-to-week, etc.

Figure 13 shows the three types of variation that are possible in a quality characteristic. A few units, generally three to five, are produced consecutively at any given time. Then some time is allowed to elapse before another three to five consecutive units are run off. The process is repeated a third time, and, if need be, a fourth or fifth time, *until at least 80% of the out-of-control variation in the process being investigated is captured.* This is an important rule in multi-vari experimentation.

By plotting the results of the multi-vari run, the variation can be determined to be positional (within unit), as in A of Figure 13, or cyclical (unit-to-unit), as in B, or temporal (time-to-time) as in C. The multi-vari chart should never be confused with a control chart. It is a snapshot in time of how variation in a process is "breathing." One can call it a stethoscope of variation. For this reason, it is the only one of the D.O.E. tools in which the running or checking sequence should not be randomized.

MULTI-VARI CASE STUDY: THE ROTOR SHAFT

A manufacturer producing cylindrical rotor shafts, with a diameter requirement of 0.0250" ± 0.001", was experiencing excessive scrap. A

Figure 13. Three types of possible variations in multi-vari charts.

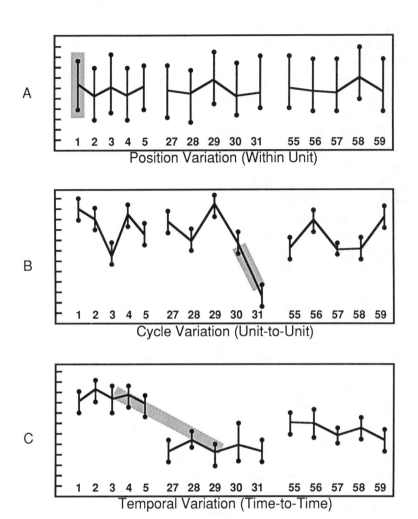

A

1 2 3 4 5   27 28 29 30 31   55 56 57 58 59
Position Variation (Within Unit)

B

1 2 3 4 5   27 28 29 30 31   55 56 57 58 59
Cycle Variation (Unit-to-Unit)

C

1 2 3 4 5   27 28 29 30 31   55 56 57 58 59
Temporal Variation (Time-to-Time)

process capability study indicated a spread of 0.0025″, against the requirement of 0.002″—i.e., a C_{pk} of 0.8. The foreman was ready to junk the old turret lathe that produced the shaft and buy a new one for $70,000 that could hold a tolerance of ± 0.0008″—i.e., a C_{pk} of 1.25. However, on the advice of a consultant, the plant manager directed that a mult-vari study be conducted before the purchase of the new lathe, even though its pay-back period would be only nine months.

Figure 14 shows the results of the multi-vari chart. The four positional (within each shaft) variations describe taper changes from the left side of each shaft to the right, and out-of-round conditions— maximum diameter and minimum diameter on each side of the shaft. The cyclical variations, from one shaft to the next, are shown by the thin connecting lines between the four readings of each shaft. The temporal variations, from one time period to the next, are also shown.

A quick glimpse reveals, even to a novice unfamiliar with multi-vari charts, that the greatest variation seems to be time-to-time, with the largest change occurring between 10 a.m. and 11 a.m. This provided the foreman with a strong clue. What generally happens around 10 a.m.? A coffee break! When the next sample of three shafts was taken at 11 a.m., the readings were very similar to those at the start of production at 8 a.m. He was now able to equate the time variations with temperature. As the day progressed, the readings got lower and lower, until there was a dramatic reversal about 10 a.m.—brought on by the machine being shut down at 10 a.m. for the coffee break. Temperature, therefore, could be a possible Red X. The foreman discovered, to his embarrassment, that the amount of coolant in the lathe tank was low. When the coolant was added to the prescribed level, the time-to-time variation, which accounted for approximately 50% of the allowed variation (specification width of 0.002), was reduced to an inconsequential figure. With one stroke—adding coolant—almost 50% of the allowed variation was eliminated!

The foreman believed that the unit-to-unit variation, accounting for about 5% of the total allowed variation, was not worth investigating. However, the within-unit positional variation showed the second-largest variation—about 10% and 30% of the allowed variation, respectively, for the taper and out-of-round conditions.

The variation in taper showed a significant nonrandom pattern, with the left side always higher than the right side. (It is important that every multi-vari chart be scanned for such nonrandom trends.) This led the foreman to conclude that the cutting tool, as it traversed the rotor shaft from left to right, was not parallel to the axis of the shaft. A slight adjustment in the setting reduced taper to almost zero. Thus another 10% of the allowed variation was virtually eliminated.

Finally, the foreman attacked the cause of the out-of-round condition in each shaft. This was traced to a worn bearing guiding

Figure 14.   The rotor shaft multi-vari chart.

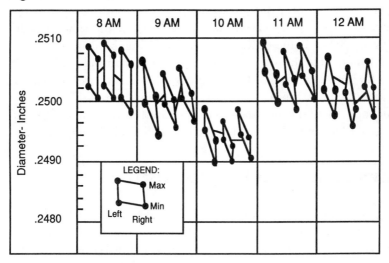

the chuck axis. New bearings were installed for a total cost of $200, including labor. This eliminated nearly 30% of the allowed variation.

Variation Type	% of Total Variation	Variation Cause	Variation Correction	% Variation Reduced
time-to-time	50%	low level of coolant	coolant added	nearly 50%
within unit	10%	nonparallel setting	setting adjustment	nearly 10%
within unit	30%	worn bearings	new bearings	nearly 30%
unit-to-unit	5%	?	—	—

In summary, the following results were achieved in the rotor shaft multi-vari study: the total variation in follow-on production was reduced from 0.0025″, down to 0.0004″, and the new C_{pk} was $0.002/0.0004 = 5.0$. The benefits: zero scrap and a cost avoidance of $70,000 through retaining the old machine.

There is a moral in this story. Too often, American industry is prone to throw out an old machine or process before investigating the underlying causes of variation, which—90% of the time—can be eliminated or reduced without the crushing burden of capital investment. The Japanese, on the other hand, painstakingly search out the causes of variation in the old machines and optimize yields. However, the techniques they use, for the most part, are brute-force methods, such as cause-and-effect diagrams, as compared with the elegant Shainin tools, of which the multi-vari is only one example.

PRACTICE EXERCISE ON MULTI-VARI CHARTS

In a multi-vari study on the adhesion of tiles mounted on a strip, the data shown below are arranged (a) within each strip; (b) strip-to-strip; and (c) time-to-time. A plot of the data is also shown (H and L are the highest and lowest adhesions, repsectively, within each strip; X is the average within each strip; 0 is the average of all three strips within each time interval.)

	\multicolumn{3}{c}{}						
\multicolumn{9}{c}{Multi-Vari Study: Tile Adhesion}								
	8:30 a.m.			1:00 p.m.			3:00 p.m.		
Strip Nos:	11	12	13	267	268	269	314	315	316
	66	59	54	60	57	47	38	14	56
	56	58	32	53	37	57	9	43	39
	58	66	59	44	46	48	54	8	60
	65	48	48	50	44	49	60	60	58
	67	63	72	58	52	56	57	38	60
Strip Avg:	62.4	58.8	53.0	53.0	47.2	51.4	43.6	32.6	54.6
Time Avg:		58.1			50.5			43.6	

Question 1. What is the family of the Red X? Justify your choice.
Question 2. What is the family of the Pink X? Justify your choice.
Question 3. What nonrandom trends do you detect?

These are the answers to the practice exercise on multi-vari charts.

Range of time variation (averages):   58.1 - 43.6 = 14.5
Range of strip-strip variation (averages):   62.4 - 32.6 = 29.8
Range of within strip variations: 60 - 8 = 52.0
        (3 p.m. strip No. 315)

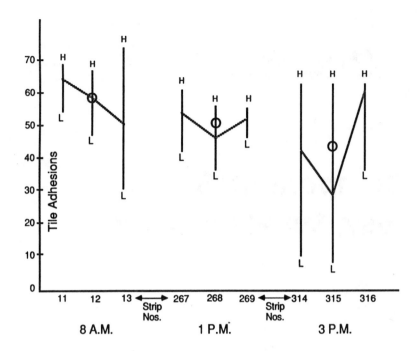

Question 1. The greatest variation (Red X family) is within strip.

Question 2. The second greatest variation (Pink X family) is strip-to-strip.

Question 3. With respect to nonrandom trends, (1) there seems to be a deterioration in adhesion with time; (2) the 3 p.m. adhesions show the greatest variation and the greatest deterioration; (3) there is a fair degree of consistency among the highest adhesions within each strip, indicating that if the root cause of the variations is determined (with follow-on variables search or full factorial experiments), a respectable adhesion between 60 and 70 can be achieved.

Chapter 7

Components Search: Easy, Sure-Fire Clues

Components search is another simple but powerful technique whereby a very large number of possible causes of variation (even over 1,000 and more) can be reduced to the family of the Red X or the Red X itself. Reduction to the lowest number of possible causes is the *objective*.

PRINCIPLE, PREREQUISITES, AND PROCEDURE

A game analogy can be used to illustrate the *principle* behind components search. The game is to ask a person to select any word in a dictionary. The object is for the "problem solver" or questioner to locate the exact page containing the selected word through "yes" or "no" responses to the problem solver's questions. The questioner starts with the middle page number in the dictionary and asks if the word is located beyond the middle page. A "yes" or "no" answer eliminates half the pages of the dictionary. The next question of a similar nature eliminates three-fourths of the dictionary pages and so on, until, by the eleventh "yes" or "no" answer, the exact page location is determined. Within another six tries, the exact location of the word within the page—and hence the word itself—can be pin-pointed.

The same principle of binary questions is used in components search, where the culprit variable can be traced from an assembly of, say, over 1,000 parts down to a subassembly of, say, 100 parts, to a sub-subassembly of 20 parts, down eventually to the Red X.

What are the *prerequisites* to components search?

- The technique is applicable, primarily, in assembly operations (but also in process-oriented operations, where there are several similar processes or machines), where good and bad units are found.
- The performance (output) must be measurable and repeatable.
- The units must be capable of disassembly and reassembly without a significant change in the original output.
- There must be at least two assemblies or units—one good and one bad.

The *procedure* to be followed in components search involves ten steps.

1. Select a good unit and a bad unit (preferably drawn at random from a sufficient number of good and bad units).

2. Determine the quantitative parameter by which good and bad units are to be measured. Measure both units and note the readings.

3. Disassemble the good unit, reassemble and remeasure it. Disassemble the bad unit, reassemble and remeasure it. If the difference, D, between the good and bad units exceeds the repeatability difference, d, within each unit by a minimum ratio of 5:1, a significant and repeatable difference between the good and bad units is established. (See Case Study.)

4. Based upon engineering judgment, rank the likely component problems, within a unit, in descending order of perceived importance.

5. Switch the top-ranked component from the good unit or assembly with the corresponding component in the bad assembly. Measure the two assemblies.

6(a). If there is no change, i.e., if the good assembly stays good and the bad assembly stays bad, the top component, A, is unimportant. Go to component B.

  (b). If there is a partial change in the two assembly outputs, A is not the only imporant variable. A could be a Pink X family. Go to Component B.

  (c). If there is a complete reversal in the outputs of the two assemblies, A could be in the Red X family. There is no further need for components search.

7. In each of the three alternatives in Step 6, restore component A to the original good and bad units (before Step 5) to assure that the original condition is repeated. Repeat Steps 5 and 6 with the next most important component, B, then C, then D, etc., if the results in each component swap are 6(a) or 6(b).

8. Ultimately, the Red X family will be indicated if there is complete reversal with a single component. Alternatively, there may be two or more Pink X and Pale Pink X families of components if there are two or more partial reversals.

9. With the important variables identified, a capping run of these important variables banded together in the good and bad assemblies must be conducted to verify their importance.

10. Finally, a factorial matrix, using the data generated in Steps 6, 7, and 8, is drawn to determine, quantitatively, main effects and interaction effects. Steps 9 and 10 are best explained using a real-life case study.

COMPONENTS SEARCH CASE STUDY: THE HOURMETER

An hourmeter, built by an electronics company, had a 20-25% defect rate because several of the units could not meet the customer's reliability requirement of perfect operation at -40°C; going down only to 0°C before malfunction.

The hourmeter consists of a solenoid cell, with a shield to concentrate the electrical charge, which pulses at regular intervals. The pulse triggers a solenoid pin, which in turn causes a verge arm, or bell crank, to trip the counter, advancing it by one unit. The counter is attached to a numeral shaft containing numeral wheels. These numeral wheels are separated from each other by idler gears, which rotate on an idler gear shaft. Both the idler gear shaft and the numeral shaft are attached to the main frame, made of hard white plastic. The pulsing rhythm is provided by an electronics board.

Establishing Significant Repeatable Differences

	High *(good) assembly*	*Low* *(bad) assembly*
Initial results	O.K. at (H1): -40°C	(L1): 0°C
Results after disassembly and reassembly	O.K. at (H2): -35°C	(L2): -5°C

The test for a significant and repeatable difference between the good units and bad units is determined by the formula:

$$D: d \geq 5:1$$

i.e., the ratio of D to d should be a minimum of 5:1; where: D = the difference between good and bad assembly averages, i.e.,

$$D = \frac{H1 + H2}{2} - \frac{L1 + L2}{2}$$

and d = the average difference in repeatability among the good and bad assemblies, i.e.,

$$d = \frac{H1 - H2}{2} + \frac{L1 - L2}{2}$$

In the above replication:

$$D = \frac{-40° + (-35°)}{2} - \frac{(0°) + (-5°)}{2} =$$

$(-37.5°) - (2.5°) = -35°$

$$d = \frac{-40° - (-35°)}{2} + \frac{(0°) - (-5°)}{2} =$$

$(-2.5°) + (-2.5°) = -5°$

Therefore D:d = 35°:5° = 7:1, which meets the 5:1 rule.

Ranking of Components by Importance

(Engineering Judgment)

Rank	Components	Label
1	Solenoid, pin and shield	A
2	Idler gear shaft	B
3	Numeral shaft	C
4	Main frame	D
5	Bell crank	E
6	Idler gears	F
7	Numeral wheels	G
8	Circuit board	H
9	Remainder of components	R (Remainder)

Testing Symbols

$A_L R_H =$ A from low (bad) unit, with remainder of components, R, from high (good) unit

$A_H R_L =$ A from high (good) unit, with remainder of components, R, from low (bad) unit

etc. . . .

Capping Run

This is a concluding test, where the high (good) levels of the important variables are tested with the low (bad) levels of the remaining variables—and vice versa—to see if a complete reversal takes place. If it does, the important variables are captured, and the remainder, as a group, can be reduced in cost.

Test Results

After initial and replication tests, each component is swapped, one at a time, between high (good) and low (bad) assemblies.

Test No.	Component Switched	"High" Assembly	Results	"Low Assembly"	Results
Initial	—	All Comp. High	-40°	All Comp. Low	0°
Disassembly & Reassembly	—	All Comp. High	-35°	All Comp. Low	-5°
1	A	$A_L R_H$	-40°	$A_H R_L$	-5°
2	B	$B_L R_H$	-35°	$B_H R_L$	0°
3	C	$C_L R_H$	-35°	$C_H R_L$	-5°
4	D	$D_L R_H$	-20°	$D_H R_L$	-5°
5	E	$E_L R_H$	-40°	$E_H R_L$	0°
6	F	$F_L R_H$	-40°	$F_H R_L$	-5°
7	G	$G_L R_H$	-20°	$G_H R_L$	-5°
8	H	$H_L R_H$	-35°	$H_H R_L$	0°
Capping Run	D & G	$D_L G_L R_H$	0°	$D_H G_H R_L$	-40°

Figure 15 is a graphical representation of the test results. It shows the clear separation between the original high (good) and low (bad) assemblies, as well as their replicated versions (disassembled and reassembled). The graph shows a partial convergence between the high and low assemblies when components D (main frame) and G (numeral wheels) are switched. The contribution of the remaining components is minor or zero.

In the capping run, when the two Pink X components—D and G—are combined at low levels, with all other components at high levels, the results are bad. When D and G are combined at high levels, with all other components at low levels, the results are good. The graph shows a complete reversal of high and low—indicating that the family of the Red X is narrowed down to D and G; that all other components are unimportant; that further components search can be discontinued; and that the tolerances of the remaining components can be opened up.

FACTORIAL ANALYSIS

The purpose of a factorial analysis is to determine, quantitatively, the importance of each major factor, previously identified in a com-

Figure 15. Components search: hour meter case study.

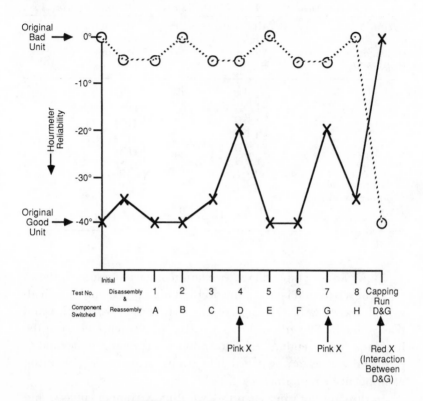

ponents search, variables search, or full factorial experiment, and to quantify the interaction effects between such factors as they affect a desired output.

Main Effects and Interaction Effects. Before a factorial analysis can be explained, it is necessary to understand main effects and interaction effects. A simple analogy will help. Take two numbers, 3 and 7.

Added together, their sum is 10. Numbers 3 and 7 can be called independent variables, each contributing independently to the result of 10, which can be called a main effect. However, 3 + 7 can also produce a different number in the physical world (though not in mathematics), like 16, where the whole is greater than the sum of the parts. This is called an interaction effect, which is additive. There is a synergy, a symbiotic relationship between the two independent variables 3 and 7.

On the other hand, 3 + 7 can also result in a lower number, like 2. This is also an interaction effect, but is subtractive. The two independent variables 3 and 7 tend to oppose and cancel one another. It can be pictured in this way.

Independent Variables	Result	Type of Effect
3 + 7	10	Main Effect
3 + 7	16	Interaction Effect - Additive
3 + 7	2	Interaction Effect - Subtractive

There are many examples of interaction effects. For instance, alcohol alone and drugs alone may not necessarily create lasting injury (unless taken in excess); but if a person takes both at the same time, the result can be fatal. That is an interaction effect. Another example would be hydrogen and oxygen. Strike a match in either by itself and nothing happens. But with the right mixture of the two, an explosion will occur when the match is lit. This phenomenon is a classical example of an interaction effect. In the world of human relations, there are similar interaction effects. Ordinary people, working and pulling together, often achieve extraordinary results. The world of sports, where teams have been "fired up," often have additive interaction effects. On the other hand, in the field of politics and in industry, with people "bucking" one another, we see almost a checkmate condition due to subtractive interaction effects.

In the design of experiments it is necessary not only to quantify the main effects of each important factor, but also the interaction effects between these important factors or variables. This is best done in a factorial analysis, as shown in Figure 16 for the components search in the hourmeter case study.

Because component D, the main frame, and component G, the numeral wheels, are the only two factors that showed a partial reversal during components search and a full reversal when switched together, they can be called Pink X factors by themselves and a Red X in combination. The evidence is strong that there is a significant interaction between components D and G.

To quantify the main and interaction effects of factors D and G, the matrix in Figure 16 must be drawn up. First, the outputs when

Figure 16. Factorial analysis.

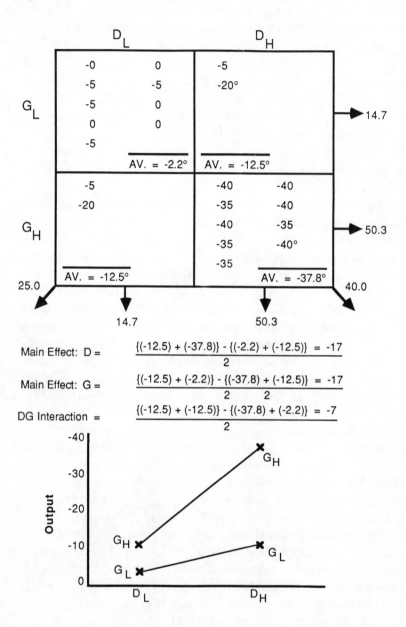

Main Effect: D = $\dfrac{\{(-12.5) + (-37.8)\} - \{(-2.2) + (-12.5)\}}{2} = -17$

Main Effect: G = $\dfrac{\{(-12.5) + (-2.2)\} - \{(-37.8) + (-12.5)\}}{2 \qquad 2} = -17$

DG Interaction = $\dfrac{\{(-12.5) + (-12.5)\} - \{(-37.8) + (-2.2)\}}{2} = -7$

both D and G are low should be entered from the test results. The first reading, 0°, is from the initial "low assembly," where D and G are both "low." The second, -5°, is from the replicated low assembly. The third, fourth, and fifth readings of -5°, 0°, and -5° are from the low assemblies in tests 1, 2, and 3, as are the seventh, eighth, and tenth readings of 0°, -5°, and 0° from the low assemblies in tests 5, 6, and 8. The last test where D and G are both low is in the capping run (with R_H - remaining components high). That reading is 0°. In similar fashion, there are two readings where D is high and G is low; two readings where D is low and G is high; and nine readings where both D and G are high. The average for each cell is then calculated.

In the factorial matrix of Figure 16, if the averages in the D_L column are added up and those in the D_H column also added, the difference between these additions divided by 2 gives the contribution of factor D alone to the output. This is because, in the addition of the two D_L and D_H columns, G_L and G_H balance one another (or cancel out). This is called the main effect of factor D. Similarly, adding up the averages in the G_L and G_H rows and dividing their difference by 2 gives the contribution of factor G alone. Here D_L and D_H balance one another. This is called the main effect of factor G. Finally, when the averages in the diagonal from cell $D_H G_L$ to $D_L G_H$ are added and the averages in the diagonal from cell $D_L G_L$ to $D_H G_L$ are also added, the difference between these additionals divided by 2 gives the contribution of the D and G interaction alone to the output.

Figure 16 also shows a graphical plot of the D-G interaction effect. The $G_L D_L$ reading of -2.2° is plotted as are the remaining three readings of $D_L G_H$ at -12.5°, $D_H G_L$ at -12.5°, and $D_H G_H$ at -37.8°. When these four points are connected by two lines, G_L and G_H, there is a nonparallel effect indicating the presence of a reasonably strong interaction between factors D and G. (If the lines had been parallel, the interpretation would be that D and G produce main effects only with no interaction present.)

THE FINAL SOLUTION TO THE HOUR METER CASE STUDY

Table 9 is a summary of the final solution to which components search pointed the way. *As a result, the defect rate went from the 20-25% range down to zero!*

Table 9. Final solution to hour meter case study.

ANALYSIS OF EXPERIMENT

- Main frame and numeral wheels causing drop in performance

ENGINEERING ANALYSIS

- 60 x life-size model built
- Isolated *first* numeral wheel and main frame as problem
- Made measurements at critical points at different temperatures

RESULTS

- Main frame shrunk by up to 0.002″ bringing numeral wheel and idler shaft too close
- First numeral wheel off center by 0.005″
- Counter jammed when shrinkage coincided with eccentricity

SOLUTION

- Redesign main frame (cost $50,000)
- *Or* change numeral wheel specification and tolerance (low cost)
- Second alternative selected

POSTSCRIPT

- Yields rose from 75-80% to 100%

The reliability engineer, who conducted the components search study, wrote the following postscript to his report.

The problem had been with us for 18 months. We had talked to suppliers; we had talked to engineers and designers; we had talked to engineering managers; *but we never talked to the parts. With the components search technique, we identified the problem in just three days!*

PRACTICE EXERCISE ON COMPONENTS SEARCH: TIME DELAY

An electronic instrument has a problem of a long time delay between the "power on" signal and when the unit actually starts to function. A "good" unit has a time delay of around 16 milli-seconds (m.s.), while a "bad" unit has one of 30 m.s. The oscillator circuit containing ten components was the source of the delay. The following components search was conducted. (R=Rest of assembly).

Test No.	Component Switched	High Assembly	Results (m.s.)	Low Assembly	Results (m.s.)
Initial	—	All Comp. High	13	All Comp. Low	34
Disassembly & Reassembly	—	All Comp. High	16	All Comp. Low	38
1	A = Crystal	$A_L R_H$	16	$A_H R_L$	19
2	B = Microprocessor	$B_L R_H$	16	$B_H R_L$	35
3	C = Transistor	$C_L R_H$	14	$C_H R_L$	33
4	D = Capacitor C_2	$D_L R_H$	15	$D_H R_L$	37
5	E = Capacitor C_1	$E_L R_H$	16	$E_H R_L$	18
Capping Run	A & E	$A_L E_L R_H$	32	$A_H E_H R_L$	17

Question 1. Determine if there is a significant and repeatable difference between the high and low assemblies in the initial and replicated (after disassembly and assembly) tests. Use the D:d $\geq$ 5:1 ratio test.

Question 2. Plot the results in the above table. What are the important components? Is there a Red X (complete reversal)? Are there Pink Xs (partial reversal)? Was the capping run successful (complete reversal)?

Question 3. Construct a factorial analysis. Determine the main and interaction effects of the important components.

Question 4. Construct a graphical plot to show the extent of interaction.

The answers to the exercise on components search follow:

Question 1. $D = (13 + 16)/2 - (34 + 38)/2 = 21.5$
$d = (13 - 16)/2 + (34 - 38)/2 = 3.5$ (absolute values only)
$D:d = 21.5/3.5 = 6.14$

Since the ratio is greater than 5, there is a significant and repeatable difference.

Question 2. The graph above shows that components A and E—the crystal and capacitor C_1—are two Pink Xs (partial reversal), indicating an additive interaction effect. The capping run is successful—a Red X—showing complete reversal.

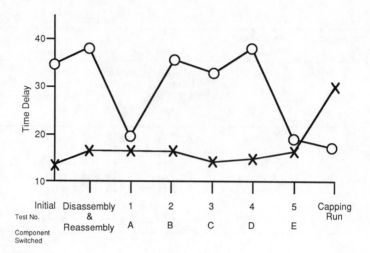

It was determined that the capping run was successful. Use factorial analysis and determine the contrasts. What are your conclusions?

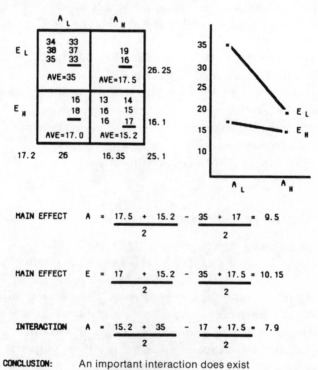

	A_L	A_H	
E_L	34 33 38 37 35 33 AVE=35	19 16 AVE=17.5	26.25
E_H	16 18 AVE=17.0	13 14 16 15 16 17 AVE=15.2	16.1
	17.2 26	16.35 25.1	

MAIN EFFECT $A = \dfrac{17.5 + 15.2}{2} - \dfrac{35 + 17}{2} = 9.5$

MAIN EFFECT $E = \dfrac{17 + 15.2}{2} - \dfrac{35 + 17.5}{2} = 10.15$

INTERACTION $A = \dfrac{15.2 + 35}{2} - \dfrac{17 + 17.5}{2} = 7.9$

CONCLUSION: An important interaction does exist
as well as two important main effects:

Question 3. The factorial analysis shows that factors A and E contribute 9.5 m.s. and 10.15 m.s., respectively, to the total variations in delay, while the A - E interaction contributes 7.9 m.s.

Question 4. The graphical plot shows a strong interaction (nonparallel response) between A & E.

The above exercise is based on an actual case study. Engineering investigation revealed that the series impedance of the crystal was on the low side and the capacitor leakage on the high side. When this condition was present in both components, the oscillator circuit loaded down the microprocessor, causing a long time delay. Working with the capacitor supplier (using D.O.E.), the conductors of the components search were able to reduce leakage, at no extra cost, and to resolve the time delay.

Chapter 8

Paired Comparisons: The Detective Method

OBJECTIVE, APPLICATION, PROCEDURE

The paired comparisons method is very similar to components search, with the same objective: reducing a large number of possible causes of variation down to the family of the Red X by providing clues derived from comparisons of paired good and bad units.

The technique is used when:

- Components or subassemblies in units cannot be disassembled or reassembled (unlike components search).
- When there are several good and bad units that can be paired.
- When a suitable parameter can be found to distinguish good from bad.

The technique is applicable in assembly work or processes or in test equipment, where there are similar units, work stations, or instruments, respectively. It is also a powerful tool in failure analysis.

The procedure to be followed in paired comparisons involves five steps:

1. Select one good unit and one bad unit (drawn, where possible, at random from a sufficient number of good and bad units).
2. Call this pair one. Observe and note differences between these two units. The differences can be visual, dimensional, electrical, mechanical, chemical, etc. The observation techniques could involve the eye, X-rays, scanning electron microscopes, test-to-destruction, etc.
3. Select a second pair of good and bad units. Observe and note the differences, as in Step 1.
4. Repeat this search process with a third, fourth, fifth, and sixth pair—until the observed differences show a pattern of repeatability.
5. Usually, by the fifth or sixth pair, the observed differences will repeat themselves, providing a strong clue for the major cause of variation.

PAIRED COMPARISONS CASE STUDY: THE FAILED DIODE

A DO-35-diode, used in an under-the-hood electronics module in an automobile, had an unacceptable failure rate. Several of the failed diodes were brought back from the field and compared against good units that had no flaws. The results of the paired comparisons, when examined under a scanning electron microscope, were as follows.

Pair No.		Observed Differences
1. Good-Bad	Good:	no flaws
	Bad:	chipped die; oxide defects; copper migration
2. Good-Bad	Good:	no flaws
	Bad:	alloying irregularities; oxide defects
3. Good-Bad	Good:	no flaws
	Bad:	oxide defects; contamination
4. Good-Bad	Good:	no flaws
	Bad:	oxide defects; chipped die

Conclusion: 1. 4 repeats in oxide defects - probable Red X family
2. 2 repeats in chipped die - probable Pink X family

Solution: Working with the semiconductor supplier (who, up to this analysis, had resisted responsibility), the following corrective actions were instituted.

1. For oxide defects:
   - thicker photo resist
   - mask inspection
   - increased separation between mask and die
2. For chipped die:
   - reduced oxide thickness in scribe grid

PRACTICE EXERCISE ON PAIRED COMPARISONS: CRYSTAL DROP TEST

A 12 MHZ crystal was failing to meet a reliability requirement when subjected to a drop test from a height of one meter. Several failed samples were collected and compared against good crystals (which had passed the drop test) for external differences. None was found. It was decided, then, to x-ray each pair of good and bad units, with the following results.

Pair No.		*Observed Differences*
1. Good-Bad	Good:	Straight post
	Bad:	Post tilted 10° from vertical
2. Good-Bad	Good:	Straight post
	Bad:	Post tilted 5° from vertical
3. Good-Bad	Good:	Straight post
	Bad:	Post tilted 20° from vertical
4. Good-Bad	Good:	Straight post
	Bad:	Post tilted 10° from vertical

Question 1. What is the observable, repeatable difference between the good and bad crystals?

Question 2. Does the difference need to be validated by further tests?

These are the answers to the exercise on paired comparisons:

Question 1. The observable difference is obvious—tilted posts.

Question 2. A B vs. C test (see Chapter 11) was set up to determine if preselected crystals with straight posts (B units) would outperform preselected crystals with tilted posts (C units) in further drop tests. The result: the crystals with tilted posts all failed within 1 meter in drop tests. The crystals with straight posts did not fail even up to 2 meters.

The solution was that a new automated crystal assembler was used by the crystal supplier to properly frame the mounting post of the crystal base and insert the crystal wafer.

Chapter 9

Variables Search: The Rolls Royce of Variation Reduction

The systematic reduction of variation starts with a multi-vari chart, a components search, or a paired comparison, where the aim is to reduce a very large number of unrelated causes down to a smaller family of related causes, generally five to fifteen. Variables search is the next step. Its *objective* is to: (1) pinpoint the Red X, Pink X, and, sometimes, one to three more interacting variables (it being quite possible that a strong interaction between two variables may itself be the Red X or Pink X); and (2) separate the important variables from the unimportant ones; tightly control the former; and open up the tolerances on the latter so as to reduce costs.

PRINCIPLE AND APPLICATION

One of the important principles in D.O.E. is to design an experiment so that every variable is tested with each level of every other variable. As an example, if 8 variables are the possible causes in the variation of a given output, and two levels of each variable are considered, there are 2^8 or 256 combinations of possible tests. Only a full factorial experiment (explained in Chapter 10) can test all these combinations. But a full factorial with 256 experiments would be very costly and time-consuming. Hence various shortcuts have been applied, such as the fractional factorial design in the classical approach and the orthogonal array in the Taguchi approach. However, as stated earlier, both these approaches have such a hit-and-miss method of selecting only a few combinations, such as 16 or 32, out of the total of 256, that the results are modest and often inaccurate.

Variables search overcomes this difficulty *by a homing-in binary technique—through a process of elimination.* The *principle* is similar to that explained in components search. In fact, the second stage of a variables search experiment is a components search. Thus, 256 or 512 or 1,024 or 2,048 combinations can be reduced to yield Red X or Pink X culprits in 20, 22, 24, or 26 experiments! It is small wonder that variables search is called the Rolls Royce of D.O.E. techniques.

Variables search is most *applicable* when there are 5 or more variables to investigate. While there is no theoretical upper limit, practical considerations limit the number of variables to 20. Further, the output must be measurable—a variable, preferably, although attributes can be used as well. Finally, in the choice of "best" and "worst" levels, it is advisable to know and to quantify "best" and "worst" in advance. This is explained in the procedure below.

PROCEDURE IN VARIABLES SEARCH

Stage 1

1. List the most important input variables, or factors, A, B, C, D, E, F, G, H, and so on, in descending order of importance of each factor's ability to influence the output. This is based on engineering judgment, although such judgment can be—and often is—wrong.
2. Assign two levels to each factor—a best (B) that is most likely to contribute to good results and a worst (W) that is likely to give poor results. (The choice of the worst level should be based on realism and reasonableness, not some outlandish value that guarantees total failure.)

3. Run two experiments, one with all factors at their best levels, the other with all factors at their worst levels. Run two more experiments* at the best and worst levels to assess residual and experimental error.

4. Apply the D:d ≥ 5:1 rule, as seen in the components search case study, where D is the difference between the average of the best readings and worst readings; and d is the average of the differences in repeatability within each best and worst pair of readings, added together, i.e.,

$$D = \frac{B1 + B2}{2} - \frac{W1 + W2}{2}$$
$$d = \frac{(B1 - B2) + (W1 - W2)}{2}$$

5. If the difference in outputs (D) between levels is greater than the difference in outputs within each level (d) by a minimum of a 5:1 ratio, the Red X is captured as being one or more of the factors considered in Step 1.

6. If the ratio is less than 5:1, the right factors were not chosen in Step 1 or the levels used for one or more factors may have been reversed between "best" and "worst." The experimental team conducting the variables search should not be discouraged if this happens, because engineering judgment is frequently wrong. In such an event, there are three alternatives to pursue:

   (a) If the team feeling is that the wrong factors were selected in Step 1, decide on new factors and rerun Stage 1.

   (b) If the team feeling is that the right factors were selected, but the levels of some of these factors were mistakenly reversed between "best" and "worst," run B vs. C tests on each suspicious factor to see whether the best and worst levels are reversed or not. (B vs. C tests are explained in Chapter 11.)

   (c) A third method might be to try the selected factors, four at a

---

*A newer rule suggests yet another two experiments. Then rank the "best" and "worst" levels in the six experiments in descending order of desired output. If the three "best" levels outrank the three "worst" levels, there is 95% confidence that the best levels are significantly better than the worst levels and that the Red X is captured.

time, using full factorial experiments (see Chapter 10) to determine important and unimportant factors.

Stage 2

1. Run an experiment with the worst level of the most important factor, A, i.e., A_W, along with the best levels of the remaining factors—labeled R_B. Measure the result of the $A_W R_B$ combination.

   (a) If there is no change from the *best* results in Step 3 of Stage 1, the top factor A is unimportant.

   (b) If there is a partial change from the worst results in Step 3 of Stage 1—in the direction of the test results—A is not the only important factor or variable. A could be a Pink X along with another factor.

   (c) If there is a complete reversal, where the *worst* results in Step 3 of Stage 1 are approximated, A is the Red X.

2. Run a second experiment with the best level of A, i.e., A_B, along with the worst levels of the remaining factors—labeled R_W. Measure the result of the $A_B R_W$ combination.

   (a) If there is no change from the *worst* results in Step 3 of Stage 1, the top factor A is further confirmed as unimportant.

   (b) If there is a partial change from the best results in Step 3 of Stage 1—in the direction of the worst results—A is further confirmed as not the only important factor or variable.

   (c) If there is a complete reversal, where the *best* results in Step 3 of Stage 1 are approximated, A is further confirmed as the Red X and no further experimentation need be conducted.

3. Perform the same components search swap of Steps 1 and 2, sequentially, on factors B, C, D, E, F, G, H, and so on, and separate the important factors from the unimportant ones.

4. If there is not a single Red X factor, but two or three Pink X factors that display a partial change, as in 1 (b) above, perform a capping run or validation experiment with these Pink X factors at their best levels and the remaining unimportant factors at their worst levels. The results should approximate the best results of Step 3, Stage 1.

5. Next run another capping run with these Pink X factors at their

worst levels and the remaining unimportant factors at their best levels. The results should approximate the worst results of Step 3, Stage 1.

6. Finally, draw up a factorial analysis using the data generated in Stage 1 and Stage 2—similar to the technique explained in the case study on components search (Chapter 7)—to quantify the main effects and interaction effects of the important factors.

7. Make every attempt to maintain the important factors at their best levels when production starts (or for subsequent production runs) by:

   (a) Reducing and controlling supplier variability of the important components (and simultaneously getting a price decrease from the supplier based on his higher yields).

   (b) Redesigning, reducing, and controlling process variability of the important components.

   (c) Maintaining reduced process variability through positrol (see Chapter 13)

8. Conduct further experiments—scatter plots (Chapter 12) or evolutionary optimization (E.V.O.P.) (1) to determine how far the tolerances of the unimportant components can be opened—especially if there is an appreciable cost reduction benefit; (2) to find the optimum center of values for the important components and the maximum tolerances permissible, to achieve a minimum of C_{pk} of 2 for the output.

USES OF VARIABLES SEARCH

In such cases where variations or defects exist in only a small percentage of units, a single unit each for best and worst is not enough. A sufficient number of units must be tested, both for best and worst combinations, to obtain a significant difference in the percentages between best and worst. This holds true both for Stage 1 and Stage 2.

Where disassembly is not possible, the Stage 1 procedure is not changed. But in Stage 2 the sample size may have to be increased and brand-new units used for the $A_W R_B$, $A_B R_W$ combinations, etc. Although this may not give as accurate a result as a direct interchange, the main and interaction effects will still show up in a very pronounced manner.

To summarize, variables search:

- Reduces product/process variability far more than the classical approach or the Taguchi approach to the design of experiments, and also gives more dependable, repeatable results.
- Is an ideal D.O.E. tool for separating the important variables from the unimportant ones. By closely controlling the important variables, it goes beyond zero defects toward zero variation, with tremendous savings in the costs of poor quality. By opening up tolerances on the unimportant variables, it is a powerful cost-reduction tool.
- Utilizes a method so simple that it can be performed by technicians and line workers with little statistical knowledge.
- Economizes the cost of experimentation by factors of 3:1 and up to 10:1 over classical and Taguchi D.O.E. experiments.

VARIABLES SEARCH CASE STUDY: THE PRESS BRAKE

In a metal stamping/forming operation, parts produced on the press brakes could not be held to a $\pm 0.005''$ tolerance (or process width of $0.010''$). Tolerances as high as $\pm 0.010''$ were being measured some of the time in production. The press brake was perceived to be a temperamental operation—in the "black magic" category—requiring the use of highly skilled operators to get consistent results. The causes of the large variation (C_{pk}s down to 0.5) were hotly debated, answers ranging from supplier material (inconsistent thickness and/or inconsistent hardness) to press brake parameters that could not be controlled. Efforts to experiment with newer press brakes, with much higher capital costs, had not resulted in any significant quality improvement.

A variables search experiment was then tried. The objective was to bring the process under control, consistently, to $\pm 0.005''$ or closer. Six factors were selected, in descending order of perceived importance, and the best and worst levels for each factor determined. (In the interest of protecting confidential information, the precise levels used are not mentioned. They are labeled merely in general quantitative terms.) The six factors chosen together with the Stage 1 and Stage 2 results are shown in Table 10.

Table 10.   Variables search: the press brake case study.

FACTORY	BEST	WORST
A. Punch And Die Alignment	Aligned	Not Aligned
B. Metal Thickness	Thick	Thin
C. Metal Hardness	Hard	Soft
D. Metal Bow	Flat	Bowed
E. Ram Storage	Coin Form	Air Form
F. Holding Material	Level	Air Angle

Results: Numbers Are Expressed in Process Widths (i.e. 2 Times The Tolerance),
in Multiples of 0.001", Measured on 5 Units in Each Experiment

Process Widths (x 0.001")

Stage 1

	All Best Levels	All Worst Levels
Initial	4	47
Replication	4	61

D = 50;   d=7;   so D: d = 7:1 (More Than Required 5:1) So There Is a Significant, Repeatable Difference
Conclusion: Red X (or Pink X's) Captured As One Or More Of The 6 Factors

Stage 2

TEST NO.	COMBINATION	RESULTS	CONCLUSION
1	$A_W R_B$	3	A. Not Important
2	$A_B R_W$	102	
3	$B_W R_B$	5	B. Not Important
4	$B_B R_W$	47	
5	$C_W R_B$	7	C. Not Important
6	$C_B R_W$	72	
7	$D_W R_B$	23	Pink X: Interaction
8	$D_C R_W$	30	with Another Factor
9	$E_W R_B$	7	?
10	$E_B R_W$	20	
11	$F_W R_B$	73	Probable Red X + Interaction
12	$F_B R_W$	18	with Another Factor
Cappine Run	$D_W F_W R_B$	70	Complete Reversal
	$D_B F_B R_W$	4	Effected

Factorial Analysis

As a result of the variables search experiment:
- The parts tolerances on the brake could be held to ± 0.002"
  (process width of 0.004")—better than twice the original objective.

(See the case study on Components Search in Chapter 8 for a full explanation of Factorial Analysis.)

D_{BEST}		D_{WORST}	
4	3	23	
4	5	18	
	7		
4	7		
AV. = 4.9		AV. = 20.5	
73		47	102
20		61	47
			72
		70	20
AV. = 51.5		AV. = 57.8	

F BEST → 25.4

F WORST → 109.3

72.0   56.4   78.3   62.7

$$\text{Main Effect: D} = \frac{(20.5 + 51.8) - (4.9 + 51.5)}{2} = \frac{78.3 - 56.4}{2} = 10.9$$

$$\text{Main Effect: F} = \frac{(51.5 + 57.8) - (4.9 + 20.5)}{2} = \frac{109.3 - 25.4}{2} = 41.9$$

$$\text{DF Interaction} = \frac{(20.5 + 72.0) - (4.9 + 57.8)}{2} = \frac{72.0 - 62.7}{2} = 4.7$$

The above results clearly show that the Red X is factor F with a 41.9 main effect contribution to process spread. Factor D is a Pink X with a 10.9 main effect contribution to process spread and the DF interaction contributes 4.7 to process spread. The graph shoes the presence of an interaction but it is relatively weak.

- The Cp_k was increased from an unacceptable 0.5 to a comfortable 2.5 (0.010/0.004) with just one experiment.
- The material thickness and hardness were no longer thought to be important considerations and so the tolerances on these parameters could be opened up. The bow in the material was the important parameter to control.
- A fixture here was devised to keep the holding material (Red X) always level, thus eliminating operator-controlled variations.

PRACTICE EXERCISE ON VARIABLES SEARCH: ENGINE CONTROL MODULE

A microprocessor-based engine control module had to meet an important specification for idle speed current. The specification limits were from 650 m.a. to 800 m.a. There was a reject rate of 10-12% in pilot run production. Appeals to the car company for a relaxation of the specification were to no avail. If the idle speed current went below 650 m.a., the car company claimed, the car might not start. If it went above 800 m.a., some of the components could burn up.

A variables search experiment was in order. Engineering selected seven factors, in descending order of importance, that could affect the output—i.e., idle speed current. These are shown in the table below. The best levels for each factor were deemed to be at the design center value of each component. The worst levels were judged to be at one end or the other of the tolerances specified for each component. The results are also shown below.

Question 1. In Stage 1, is there a significant, repeatable difference between the best and worst levels? (Use the D:d $7 \geq 5{:}1$ test.)

Question 2. In Stage 2, identify the important and unimportant factors. Are there significant interaction effects?

Question 3. To what extent should the tolerances on the important factors be reduced?

Question 4. To what extent should the tolerances of the unimportant factors be opened up?

Question 5. Were the best and worst levels for each factor chosen correctly?

These are the answers to the exercise on variables search.

Question 1. D $= (1051.5 - 740) = 311.5$; d $= (4 + 3)/2 = 3.5$. So, D:d is much greater than the required 5:1 difference. Hence there is a significant, repeatable difference between the best and worst levels.

Question 2. The only important factor is G, the IC offset voltage. It is not only the Red X—it is a super Red X! It overshadows all the other factors put together. (Factor A may be considered to be a pale, pale Pink X.) There are virtually no interaction effects. In fact, in this example, a capping run was unnecessary.

Questions 3 and 4. The answers to Questions 3 and 4 require further experimentation. In this actual case study (where the original

FACTOR DESCRIPTION	FACTOR NOMINAL VALUE	FACTOR TOLERANCE	FACTOR LEVELS	
			BEST (B)	WORST (W)
A. RESISTOR: R85	0.68 OHMS	± 5%	0.68 OHMS	0.65 OHMS
B. POWER SUPPLY VOLTAGE : V_{CC}	5.0 VOLTS	± 5%	5.0 VOLTS	4.75 VOLTS
C. RESISTOR: R77	100 OHMS	± 1%	100 OHMS	99 OHMS
D. RESISTOR: R75	787 OHMS	± 1%	787 OHMS	729 OHMS
E. XSISTOR: Q8 SATURATION VOLTAGE	75 M.V.	150 M.V. MAX	75 M.V.	150 M.V.
F. RESISTOR: R79	43 OHMS	± 5%	43 OHMS	40.85 OHMS
G. INTEGRATED CIRCUIT: IC4	0 M.V.	± 8 M.V.	0 M.V.	-8 M.V.
OFF-SET VOLTAGE				

STAGE 1   ALL FACTORS AT BEST LEVELS   ALL FACTORS AT WORST LEVELS

742 MA   1053 MA

738 MA   1050 MA

STAGE 2	TEST NO.	COMBINATION	RESULTS (MA)	CONCLUSIONS
	1	$A_W R_B$	768	
	2	$A_B R_W$	1020	
	3	$B_W R_B$	704	
	4	$B_B R_W$	1051	
	5	$C_W R_B$	733	
	6	$C_B R_W$	1028	
	7	$D_W R_B$	745	
	8	$D_B R_W$	1018	
	9	$E_W R_B$	726	
	10	$E_B R_W$	1022	
	11	$F_W R_B$	733	
	12	$F_B R_W$	1020	
	13	$G_W R_B$	1031	
	14	$G_B R_W$	718	

Stage 1 and Stage 2 experiments were performed by a technician and completed in just two days), the IC off-set voltage tolerance was cut in half to ± 4 M.V. In negotiations with the semiconductor supplier, he was encouraged to reduce his process variability, using D.O.E. The tolerances for the two ± 1% resistors were opened up to ± 5% and the costs reduced on their procurement. The tolerances for the four remaining components were not changed, mainly because there was no price advantage for the larger tolerances. *The total savings from* *quality improvement (defects down to zero) and procurement cost reductions amounted to $450,000 in the first year alone.*

Question 5. In examining Test Numbers 3, 5, and 11 in Stage 2, the results indicate that selecting B_W, C_W, and F_W actually improved idle speed current, moving it closer to the design center of 725 m.a. Hence the best and worst levels for these three factors should have been reversed.

Chapter 10

Full Factorials: A Workhorse in the Design of Experiments

In full factorial experiments, the *objectives* are to:

- Pinpoint the most important variables—Red X, Pink X— following the homing-in techniques of multi-vari charts, components search, or paired comparisons.
- Separate and quantify the main and interaction effects of the important variables.
- Start the process of opening up tolerances on the unimportant variables.

These objectives are similar to those for variables search. The main difference is that full factorials are used to investigate four or fewer variables, whereas in variables search the number is five or more. In attempting to identify the causes of variation, engineers often cannot think of more than four causes. Alternatively, previous homing-in techniques may have reduced such causes to four or less. As a result, the full factorial technique has become a powerful workhorse in D.O.E. and, except for variables search, is used more frequently than other D.O.E. tools.

PRINCIPLE

The power in full factorials is that every one of the four (or less) chosen variables is tested with all levels (generally two) of every other variable. Thus all possible combinations of factors and levels are tested, allowing for the systematic separation and quantification of all main effects, as well as all interaction effects—including second-order interaction effects—i.e., two main variables interacting with one another; third-order interaction effects—i.e., three main variables interacting with one another; and fourth-order interaction effects— i.e., four main variables interacting with one another.

In full factorials, an investigation involving two factors and two levels is called a 2^2 factorial. An investigation involving three factors and two levels is called a 2^3 factorial. And an investigation involving four factors and two levels is called a 2^4 factorial. In this briefing, a 2^4 full factorial will be explained, since 2^2 and 2^3 factorials are simpler versions of the 2^4 factorial.

With four factors, each with two levels, there are 2^4 or sixteen combinations; hence sixteen experiments are required. In order to overcome residual error inherent in all experimentation, these sixteen experiments should be repeated (or replicated), making a total of thirty-two experiments. (A technique using end-counts and overlaps can reduce the number of experiments to sixteen, but is not discussed here in the interests of brevity.)

The sample size in each combination of factors (called cells) need be no more than one to five for variables data, but must be large enough in attribute data to be able to distinguish one cell output from another. As an example, if the objective is to detect a 5% problem and reduce it, the sample size in each cell would have to be increased to 100 units in order to differentiate between various percent defectives in each cell.

Finally, the sequence of testing should not be done in a methodical, predictable manner, *but in a random order*. This allows numerous causes not included in the experiment an equal opportunity of entering or leaving the experiment. The random order of testing can be determined through a random number table, described in most texts on statistics and quality control. For instance, if the sixteen combinations or cells are labeled sequentially and a table of random numbers selects sixteen random numbers as shown below, the sequence of testing would follow the random numbers from low to high as follows:

Cell No: 1   2   3   4   5   6   7   8   9 10 11 12 13 14 15 16
Random Nos: 38 68 83 24 86 59 40 47 20 60 43 85 25 96 93 45
Testing
Sequence: 4 11 12   2 14   9   5   8   1 10   6 13   3 16 15   7

PROCEDURE (FOR A 2^4 FACTORIAL)

1. Select the four factors to be investigated, based on previous homing-in experiments and/or engineering judgment. Designate them A, B, C, and D.
2. Determine two levels for each factor. The first level, labeled (−), is usually, but not necessarily, the current level for that factor. The second level, labeled (+), is assumed to produce better results, but, again, not necessarily so.
3. Draw up a matrix (see Table 11, Full factorials: wave solder case study) showing the sixteen combinations by which each factor is tested with each level of every other factor.
4. Randomize the sequence of testing each combination (or cell).
5. Run an experiment with each combination in the sequence indicated by the random order table and record the output in each cell.
6. Repeat Steps 4 and 5 using *another* random order for the second test sequences.
7. Calculate the average of the two readings in each cell.
8. For the thirty-two sets of readings, add all* the average readings in those cells where A is (−) and all the average cell readings where A is (+). The difference between A(−) and A(+) is due to factor A alone, because all other factors—B, C, and D—balance one another (or cancel one another). Similarly, add all the average cell readings where B is (−) and where B is (+). The difference is due to factor B alone. In like manner, calculate the

---

*The novice user of full factorials is tempted to select a single combination (cell) of factors that appears to produce the best output. This is a suboptimal solution. It ignores valuable data in the remaining fifteen cells. By looking at eight cells where a factor is (−) and eight where it is (+) we get a magnifying effect that permits a better determination of the appropriate level for each factor and the relationships between main effects and interaction effects.

Table 11. Full factorials: wave solder case study.

Product EEC IV - Model 2201
CAL No. New Machine Electrovert 337-12

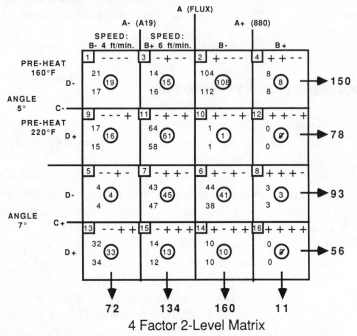

4 Factor 2-Level Matrix

A- = 72 + 134 = 206 ⎱ A- Is Worse Than A+ By 35 Defects.
A+ = 160 + 11 = 171 ⎰

B- = 72 + 160 = 232 ⎱ B- Is Worse Than B+ By 87 Defects.
B+ = 134 + 11 = 145 ⎰

C- = 150 + 78 = 228 ⎱ C- Is Worse Than C+ By 79 Defects.
C+ = 93 + 56 = 149 ⎰

D- = 150 + 93 = 243 ⎱ D- Is Worse Than D+ By 109 Defects.
D+ = 78 + 56 = 134 ⎰

(-) A19 FLUX (+) (880)
(-) 4' SPEED (+) 6'
(-) 5° ANGLE (+) 7°
(-) 160° PRE-HEAT (+) 220°

difference between the C(−) and C(+) average readings and the D(−) and D (+) average readings.

9. Construct an analysis of variance (ANOVA) table. The procedure is explained in detail, using the following case study.

FULL FACTORIALS: THE WAVE SOLDER CASE STUDY

The purpose of a wave solder process is to solder electronic components to a printed circuit (p.c.) board. Prior to this process, components are machine-inserted onto a p.c. board. The assembly is then put on a belt conveyor and passed, first, through a pre-heat chamber, and next given an application of flux—a chemical cleaning agent that removes oxides from the component and p.c. board leads. Finally, the assembly passes over a fountain (or wave) of molten solder at a given angle of incline at a predetermined temperature and at a predetermined speed to effect solder connections between the components and the board.

For many years, defect rates of 3% of the total number of connections had been tolerated as the best the process could achieve. In more modern measurements, this defect rate translates to 30,000 parts per million (p.p.m.). A quality improvement team was able to reduce the defect rate to 1%, or 10,000 p.p.m., by redesigning the p.c. boards and improving solderability on the p.c. boards and component leads.

The team felt that the remaining improvements had to come from the wave solder process. Multi-vari studies indicated large variations within the board, rather than board-to-board or time-to-time variations. Four possible causes were identified, requiring a full factorial 2^4 experiment. The target was to reduce the defect rate from 10,000 p.p.m. to 200 p.p.m.

Four factors and two levels for each factor were selected.

		Levels	
Letter	Factor	(−)*	(+)
A	Flux	A 19	A 880
B	Belt Speed	4 ft./min.	8 ft./min.
C	Angle of Incline	5°	7°
D	Pre-heat temperature	160°F	220°F

*The (−) levels represented current levels. The results of the experiments are shown in Table 11.

PROCEDURE FOR CONSTRUCTING AN ANOVA TABLE

An analysis of variance (ANOVA) table was constructed, as shown in Table 12. The procedure is as follows:

Table 12. Full factorials: wave solder: ANOVA table.

Cell Group	Factors				2 Factors Interactions						3 Factors Interactions				4 Factors Interaction	Output
	A	B	C	D	AB	AC	BC	AD	BD	CD	ABC	ABD	ACD	BCD	ABCD	
1	-	-	-	-	+	+	+	+	+	+	-	-	-	-	+	19
2	+	-	-	-	-	-	+	-	+	+	+	+	+	-	-	108
3	-	+	-	-	-	+	-	+	-	+	+	+	-	+	-	15
4	+	+	-	-	+	-	-	-	-	+	-	-	+	+	+	8
5	-	-	+	-	+	-	-	+	+	-	+	-	+	+	-	4
6	+	-	+	-	-	+	-	-	+	-	-	+	-	+	+	41
7	-	+	+	-	-	-	+	+	-	-	-	+	+	-	+	45
8	+	+	+	-	+	+	+	-	-	-	+	-	-	-	-	3
9	-	-	-	+	+	+	+	-	-	-	-	+	+	+	-	16
10	+	-	-	+	-	-	+	+	-	-	+	-	-	+	+	1
11	-	+	-	+	-	+	-	-	+	-	+	-	+	-	+	61
12	+	+	-	+	+	-	-	+	+	-	-	+	-	-	-	0
13	-	-	+	+	+	-	-	-	-	+	+	+	-	-	+	33
14	+	-	+	+	-	+	-	+	-	+	-	-	+	-	-	10
15	-	+	+	+	-	-	+	-	+	+	-	-	-	+	-	13
16	+	+	+	+	+	+	+	+	+	+	+	+	+	+	+	0
Main & Interaction Contribution	-35	-87	-79	-109	-211	-47	+33	-189	+115	+35	+73	+139	+127	-181	+39	

RED X
(FLUX+SPEED) ◄ (AB)

PINK X
(FLUX+PRE-HEAT) ◄ (AD)

THE (-) SIGN IN THE FACTOR A COLUMN IN THE LAST ROW INDICATES THAT A- IS WORSE THAN A+ BY 35 DEFECTS. SIMILAR SIGNS IN THE OTHER MAIN AND INTERACTION FACTORS INDICATES WHETHER THE (-) LEVEL OR (+) LEVEL IS WORSE.

1. In the "cell group" column, enter the cell numbers from Table 11.
2. In the "factors" column, enter the appropriate (−) and (+) signs for factors A, B, C, and D in cell 1. Here A, B, C, and D are all (−). The (−) and (+) signs merely indicate the levels of the factors used. Similarly, enter the appropriate (−) and (+) signs for A, B, C, and D in the remaining fifteen cells.
3. In the "output" column, enter the average of the outputs recorded in each cell from Table 11.
4. In the two factor interaction columns, multiply, *algebraically*, the signs of A and B in cell 1 and record the sign of the product in the AB column. Here, since A and B are both (−), the product sign for AB is (+). Similarly, determine the algebraic product of A and C, B and C, etc., and record them in the appropriate 2-factor interaction column.
5. Repeat the algebraic multiplications of A, B, and C; A, B, and D; etc.—up to A, B, C, and D, and record the signs in the appropriate three-factor or four-factor interaction column.
6. Repeat Steps 4 and 5 for all remaining fifteen cells.
7. In column A, add all the outputs where A is (−) and add all the outputs where A is (+). Note the difference between these two sums in the last row labeled "main and interaction effects contribution." Place a (−) sign above this entry if the A (−) sum is worse than the A(+) sum; or a (+) sign if the reverse is the case.
8. Similarly, add all the (+) and (−) outputs for each column B, C, and D, AB through CD, ABC through BCD and ABCD and note the difference in the last row, as in Step 7.
9. The last row now displays, in precise quantified form, the contribution of each main factor as well as each two-factor, three-factor, and four-factor interaction to the total variation.

Table 12 can now be interpreted as follows: The Red X is the interaction effect between A and B, i.e., between the flux and the belt speed. The Pink X is the interaction effect between A and D, i.e., between the flux and pre-heat temperature. The main effects of A, B, C, and D are relatively small compared to the interaction effects.

The last step is to plot the major interaction effects. The procedure is as follows:
1. For the AB interaction, observe the B and C columns jointly.

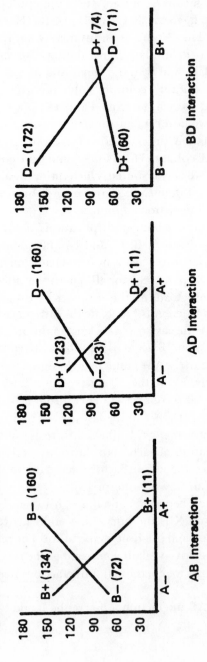

Figure 17. Interaction graph.

Add all the outputs of those cells where both B and C are (−). Add all the outputs where B is (−) and C is (+). Add the outputs where B is (+) and C is (−). Add the outputs where B is (+) and C is (+).

2. Repeat the procedure for the AD and BD interactions. The results are shown in the graph, Figure 17. All three tables show the presence of strong interactions because of nonparallel responses.

3. From the AB interaction and the AD interaction, the best results (lowest defects) occur when A is (+). This is confirmed in the last row Table 12, where A (−) is worse than A (+) by 35 defects.

4. From the AB interaction, the best results (lowest defects) occur when B is (+). This is confirmed in the last row of Table 12, where B (−) is worse than B (+) by 87 defects.

5. In the BD interaction, the best results appear to be B (−) and D (+). Yet the D (+) slope is much less steep than the D (−) slope. In such cases, the lower slope, i.e., D (+), should be chosen. The reason is that if the preferred belt speed, B (+), of 6 ft. per minute should "wander" toward B (−), or 4 ft. per minute in production, and pre-heat temperature is held at the D (−) level of 160°F, the defect level would increase rapidly—traveling along the D (−) line. Hence D (+) would be the *safer* level to use. This is further confirmed in the last row of Table 12, where D (−) is worse than D (+) by 109 defects.

Conclusion

The 2^4 factorial clearly showed that the best levels of the four factors were A (+), B (+), C (+), and D (+)—in other words, the use of the A 880 flux, the belt speed of 6 ft./minute, an incline angle of 7°, and a pre-heat temperature of 220°F. A capping run (confirmation experiment) on seventeen boards produced three defects. With 800 connections per board, the defect rate dropped to 220 p.p.m. This represented an almost 50:1 quality improvement. These are the kinds of spectacular results needed to solve problems. We must be totally discontented with 10%, 50%, or even 100% improvements. (Incidentally, neither the classical D.O.E. fraction factorials or Taguchi methods could even begin to give comparable results.)

PRACTICE EXERCISE ON FULL FACTORIALS: THE DRILLING OPERATION

In the cross-drilling of two holes, 9/64" diameter, through both walls of a piece part, a heavy exit burr and large hanging flags were present on over 50% of the parts. All shipments to date had been rejected by the customer, even after each part was blown out with high-pressure air. A 2^4 full factorial experiment was designed to optimize the parameters that could eliminate burrs and flags. Four machine parameters were selected with two levels for each factor. The (-) levels represented current production.

Factor	Levels	
	(-)	(+)
A. Spindle speed (r.p.m.)	2850	5000
B. Drill type	GT 100	Guhring Gold
C. Drill feed (in/rev.)	0.001	0.003
D. Coolant type	Water soluble Mist	Cutting oil

Output. The parts were graded for severity on a linear scale of 0 to 4.

	Scale
Minimal burr—non-defective	S0
Slight raised burr—higher than minimum	S1
Raised burr plus one hanging flag, easily broken off	S2
Raised burr plus two or more flags	S3
Excessive hanging burr and multiple flags	S4

The defect score in each cell was the number of each type of defect multiplied by the above scale.

Experiment. One hundred pieces were run in each cell combination. The sequence was randomized. A new drill was used in each experiment to eliminate the effect of tool wear. The factorial matrix and the ANOVA table are shown on the next pages (Tables 13a and 13b).

Question 1: Were 100 pieces necessary for each cell?

Question 2: What were the benefits of grading the defects on a 0-4 scale?

Table 13a. Full factorials: drill experiment: ANOVA table.

		SPINDLE SPEED A (-) : 2850 R.P.M.		A (+) : 5000 R.P.M.	
C DRILL FEED		• B(-) : GT 100	B+ : GUHRING GOLD	B (-) : GT 100	B(+) : GUHRING GOLD
C(-) 0.001	D(-) MIST	1 9 S1 : 37 S2 : 42 S3 : 13 S4 : 2 TOT: 168	2 3 S1 : 9 S2 : 26 S3 : 54 S4 : 7 TOT: 251	3 14 S1 : 42 S2 : 35 S3 : 3 S4 : 0 TOT: 121	4 5 S1 : 18 S2 : 30 S3 : 50 S4 : 0 TOT: 228
	D(+) OIL	5 11 S1 : 49 S2 : 41 S3 : 1 S4 : 2 TOT: 142	6 10 S1 : 1 S2 : 0 S3 : 1 S4 : 98 TOT: 396	7 7 S1 : 34 S2 : 42 S3 : 6 S4 : 1 TOT: 140	8 6 S1 : 3 S2 : 7 S3 : 46 S4 : 44 TOT: 331
C(+) 0.003	D(-) MIST	9 8 S1 : 50 S2 : 43 S3 : 7 TOT: 157	10 16 S1 : 15 S2 : 35 S3 : 45 S4 : 4 TOT: 236	11 12 S1 : 53 S2 : 17 S3 : 3 S4 : 0 TOT: 96	12 15 S1 : 62 S2 : 30 S3 : 2 S4 : 0 TOT: 128
	D(+) OIL	13 2 S1 : 22 S2 : 7 TOT: 36	10 16 S1 : 35 S2 : 49 S3 : 10 S4 : 1 TOT: 167	15 4 S1 : 5 S2 : 1 TOT: 7	16 1 S1 : 11 TOT: 11

QUESTION 1: Were 100 pieces necessary for each cell?
QUESTION 2: What were the benefits of grading the defects on a 0 - 4 scale?
QUESTION 3: Based on the results of a single cell, what are the best levels to use ? Why is this a poor conclusion?
QUESTION 4: From the ANOVA tables (next page), which are the Red X & Pink X factors?
QUESTION 5: What are the optimum levels to use for each factor?
QUESTION 6: Does the graphical plot for interactions confirm these choices?

*The first square in each cell corner represents the cell number. The second square in each cell represents the run sequence.

Question 3: Based on the results of a single cell, what are the best levels to use? Why is this a poor conclusion?

Question 4: From the ANOVA table, which are the Red X and Pink X factors?

Question 5: What are the optimum levels to use for each factor?

Question 6: Does the graphical plot for interactions confirm these choices?

These are the answers to the exercise questions on full factorials.

Question 1. If the defect rate had been small—5% or less—100 pieces for each cell would have been justified. With a defect rate of over 50%, a much smaller sample—say 20 units—would have been sufficient.

Table 13b. Full factorial: drill experiment: ANOVA table.

Cell Group	A	B	C	D	AB	AC	BC	AD	BD	CD	ABC	ABD	ACD	BCD	ABCD	Output
	Factors				2 Factors Interactions						3 Factors Interactions				4 Factors Interaction	
1	-	-	-	-	+	+	+	+	+	+	-	-	-	-	+	168
2	-	+	-	-	-	+	+	-	-	+	+	+	-	+	-	251
3	+	-	-	-	-	-	-	+	+	+	+	+	+	-	-	121
4	+	+	-	-	+	-	-	-	-	+	-	-	+	+	+	228
5	-	-	-	+	+	+	-	+	-	-	-	+	+	+	-	142
6	-	+	-	+	-	+	-	-	+	-	+	-	+	-	+	396
7	+	-	-	+	-	-	+	+	-	-	+	-	-	+	+	140
8	+	+	-	+	+	-	+	-	+	-	-	+	-	-	-	331
9	-	-	+	-	+	-	+	-	+	-	+	-	+	+	-	157
10	-	+	+	-	-	-	+	+	-	-	-	+	+	-	+	236
11	+	-	+	-	-	+	-	-	+	-	-	+	-	+	+	96
12	+	+	+	-	+	+	-	+	-	-	+	-	-	-	-	128
13	-	-	+	+	+	-	-	-	-	+	+	+	-	-	+	36
14	-	+	+	+	-	-	-	+	+	+	-	-	-	+	-	167
15	+	-	+	+	-	+	+	-	-	+.	-	-	+	-	-	7
16	+	+	+	+	+	+	+	+	+	+	+	+	+	+	+	11
Main & Interaction Contribution	-491	+881	-939	-155	-213	-217	-13	-389	+279	-637	-135	-167	-19	-231	+7	

2 Factor Interactions

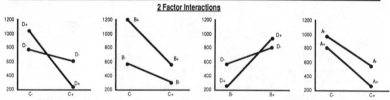

Question 2. There were two benefits to grading: (1) The defect scale was magnified. Hence differences between cells were also magnified. In fact, with the magnified scale, the sample size per cell could have been further reduced—say to 10; (2) If a particular type of defect had to be separated—e.g., burrs alone or flags alone—the matrix could easily have separated these two output categories.

Question 3. Based on a single cell, the best levels would be: A(+) B(−), C(+), D(+). As it turned out eventually, this was the best combination. Nevertheless, a full ANOVA exercise is necessary so that the very useful data contained in the remaining 15 cells is not thrown away.

Question 4. From the last row of the ANOVA table, the factor with the highest reading is C. Its best level should be C(+). The next highest factor is B. Its best level should be B(−).

Question 5. The optimum levels, based on the readings and signs in the last row of the ANOVA table, is A(+), B(−), C(+), D(+).

Question 6. The graphical plot can be interpreted as follows: In the CD interaction, C(+), D(+) give the lowest defects. Hence those are the right levels for C and D, even though the D− slope is gentler than the D+ slope. The physical rationale is that, in production, there is no danger of the coolant "wandering" to another type. Similarly in the BC interaction, the C(+), B(−) combination gives the lowest defects and the lowest slope. In the BD interaction, the B(−), D(+) combination gives the lowest defects and D(+) is chosen for the same reason as in the CD interaction. In the AC interaction, the A(+), C(+) combination gives the lowest defects and the lowest slope.

Conclusion

The results were contrary to the engineering expectations, where the lower drill feed rate was thought to be better. With the combination of higher drill feed (Red X), the Guhring Gold drill type (Pink X), the higher spindle speed, and the cutting oil, the defect rate was reduced to *zero!*

Chapter 11

B vs. C: A Versatile, Universal Tool

In B vs. C analysis, the symbols "B" and "C" stand for two processes or methods or policies that need to be compared. "C" is, generally, the current (C) process, and "B" is, supposedly, a better (B) process. But they could also be two new processes. B vs. C is a nonparametric comparative experimentation, where no assumption of normality is necessary for either the B or C process. The term "nonparametric" is a third form of data observation. In variables data, there is measurement, such as a dimension, where there can be a vast number of different readings. In attributes data, there is only "good or bad," "accept or reject." In nonparametric data, there are no measurements as in variables, but only a ranking of units—from best to worst. The power of nonparametric ranking is that it takes only a comparison between extremely small sample sizes from the two processes—often, just three from the B process and three from the C process—to assure, with a very high degree of confidence, that one is better than the other.

OBJECTIVE AND APPLICATIONS

In the design of experiments, B vs. C is generally used as a final validation of previous techniques, like multi-vari charts and variables search, that had isolated the Red X. It can also be used at the very start of design of experiments—bypassing the other techniques—but only if engineering is sure that it has a better method or design. (Given the track record of some engineers in their ability to solve problems, this is a dangerous assumption!)

In addition, B vs. C is a versatile tool that goes beyond the arena of engineering and production into almost any field—white-collar work, social services, sales, human relations, etc. It is universal in scope, simple in implementation, low in costs, and powerful in statistical effectiveness.

PRINCIPLE

Let us suppose that two processes—C, a current process, and B, a possibly better process—are to be compared. Normally, process capability studies would be run on them, with fifty to one hundred readings taken from each process. The results could be either of four frequency distributions shown in Figure 18a. If the distributions of B and C are those in (1), it is obvious that there is no difference between B and C. This is called the null hypothesis. In (2), B is generally better than C, but there is overlap, with some B units worse than some C units. We can call this a Pink X condition. In (3), the worst B units are equal to or better than the best C units—a Red X condition. In (4), the worst B units are much better than the best C units—a super Red X condition.

This kind of determination, however, would require a minimum of fifty readings drawn from each process. *The power of B vs. C tests is that with just a few units—most frequently, three B units and three C units—we can determine whether the parent populations have distributions similar to (1), (2), (3), or (4).*

The theory behind B vs. C is based on the formulas for permutations and combinations. If there are two B units and two C units, the possible ways they can be arranged in rank order (vertically) are:

Best						
↑	B	B	B	C	C	C
	B	C	C	B	B	C
	C	B	C	B	C	B
Worst	C	C	B	C	B	B

Figure 18a.   Four distributions of B and C process.

C = Current Process;   B = Better (?) Process

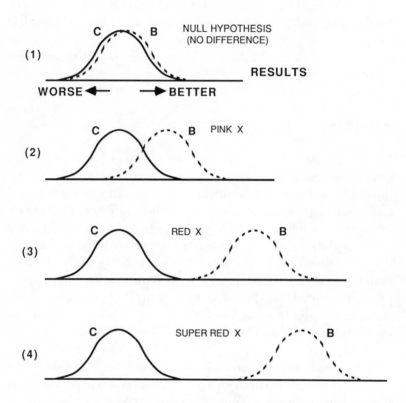

There are six ways in which two Bs and two Cs can be ranked in any order. Of these, there is only one way—out of six—in which the two Bs come out on top and the two Cs are at the bottom, by chance alone. In other words, there is a one in six, or 16.7%, risk that if two Bs come out on top and two Cs are at the bottom, it is through chance alone, but an 83.3% confidence that the B process is really better than the C process. Similarly, if there are three B units and three C units, the number of ways they can be arranged in rank order (vertically) is:

	1	2	3	4	5	6	7	8	9	10	11	12	13	14	15	16	17	18	19	20
Best	B	B	B	B	B	B	B	B	B	B	C	C	C	C	C	C	C	C	C	C
	B	B	B	C	C	C	C	C	C	C	B	B	B	B	B	B	C	C	C	C
	B	C	C	B	B	B	B	C	C	C	B	B	B	C	C	C	B	B	B	C
	C	B	C	B	B	C	C	B	B	C	B	C	C	B	B	C	B	B	C	B
	C	C	C	C	B	C	B	C	B	C	B	C	B	C	B	B	C	B	B
Worst	C	C	B	C	C	C	B	C	B	B	C	C	B	C	B	B	C	B	B	B

There are twenty ways in which three Bs and three Cs can be ranked in any order. Of these, there is only one way in which all three Bs can rank above all three Cs by chance alone. That is a 1 in 20, or 5%, chance or risk. This is known as the α risk.

The formula for the number of possible combinations $= \dfrac{(n_B + n_C)!}{n_B! \; n_C!}$

where n_B = no. of B samples

n_C = no. of C samples

! is a factorial. (As an example 8! means: $8 \times 7 \times 6 \times 5 \times 4 \times 3 \times 2 \times 1$.)

The α risk, then, is

$$\frac{1}{\text{Tot. no. of combinations}} = \frac{(n_B + n_C)!}{n_B! \; n_C!} = \frac{n_B! \; n_C!}{(n_B + n_C)!}$$

In the case of 3 Bs and 3 Cs:

the no. of combinations $= \dfrac{(3 + 3!)}{3! \; 3!} = \dfrac{6!}{3! \; 3!} =$

$$\frac{6 \times 5 \times 4 \times 3 \times 2 \times 1}{3 \times 2 \times 1 \times 3 \times 2 \times 1} = 20$$

α risk $= 1/20 = 0.05$ or 5%

The matrix below relates two decisions an experimenter can make relative to the actual, but unknown, situation.

Decision Based on Experimental Analysis	Actual (Unknown) Situation	
	B is Better Than C Yes	B is the Same as C No
B is Better Than C Yes	OK	Type I Error α Risk
B is the Same as C No	Type II Error β Risk	OK

If the experimenter decides that B is better than C (i.e., he is rejecting the null hypothesis (H_0) of B being the same as C) and B is truly better than C in the actual, but unknown, situation, the right decision was made. If, however, the actual situation contains no improvement, the experimenter will have committed a Type I error or alpha (α) risk.

If the experimenter decides that B is the same as C (i.e., he is *not* rejecting the null hypothesis) and B is truly the same as C in the actual situation, the right decision was made. If, however, the actual situation has an improvement (this is called the alternative hypothesis—H_1), the experimenter will have committed a Type II error or beta (β) risk.

The α risk, therefore, is defined as the risk of rejecting the null hypothesis—i.e., assuming improvement, when no improvement exists. The β risk is defined as the risk of accepting the null hypothesis—i.e., assuming that there is no improvement, when improvement does exist.

Table 14 is an important chart that enables the appropriate sample sizes to be selected for B vs. C tests, along with predesignated α and β risks.

PROCEDURE

Step 1: Choose an acceptable level of α risk.

There are four choices of α risks in Table 14, ranging from 0.10 to 0.001, i.e., from 10% to 0.1% risks. (Since risk plus confidence equals one, the confidence levels range from 0.90 to 0.999, i.e., from 10% to 99.9%) The α risk choice must be made *a priori*, i.e., before the fact. In most industrial situations, a *moderate* α risk of 0.10 (10%) or an *important* α risk of 0.05 (5%) is adequate. Only if the cost of the decision runs over $100,000 is the critical risk of 0.01 (1%) used. Finally, only if there is danger of large loss of life is the supercritical α risk of 0.001 (0.1%) used.

Step 2: Decide on sample sizes for B and C tests.

Table 14 contains the sample sizes for B and C tests, once the appropriate α risk is selected. There are several possible combinations. Because C is the current process, there are likely to be more C units available for testing than B units from a newer process.

Table 14. "B vs. C" sample sizes and α, β risks.

<u>α Risk: Risk Of Rejecting The Null Hypothesis (No Diff.)</u>
<u>β Risk: Risk Of Accepting Null Hypothesis When Improve-ment Exists</u>

CONSEQUENCES OF A WRONG DECISION		NOS. OF RANDOMIZED (SETS OF) TESTS		VALUES OF K (DIFFERENCE BETWEEN MEANS) β RISK =		
α RISK	CONFIDENCE	B's	C's	.50	.10	.05
0.001	0.999	2	(43)	3.90 / 3.9		4.30 / 5.5
		3	16	2.5 / 3.2		3.9 / 5.0
SUPER-CRITICAL		4	10	2.3 / 2.9		3.8 / 4.8
(LARGE LOSS OF LIFE- • FOOD POISONING • NUCLEAR REACTORS)		5	8	2.2 / 2.9		3.7 / 4.7
		6	6	2.2 / 2.8		3.7 / 4.7
0.01	0.99	2	13	2.3 / 3.0	3.4 / 4.4	3.8 / 4.6
CRITICAL		3	7	2.0 / 2.6	3.2 / 4.1	3.6 / 4.6
• A FEW LIVES LOST & • UP TO $100 MILLION		4	5	2.0 / 2.5	3.1 / 4.0	3.5 / 4.5
		5	4	2.0 / 2.5	3.1 / 4.0	3.5 / 4.5
0.05	0.95	1	19	2.5 / 3.2	3.6 / 4.6	3.9 / 5.0
IMPORTANT		2	5	1.7 / 2.2	3.0 / 3.8	3.4 / 4.3
• FOR FINDING MISTAKES IN 1 MONTH • UP TO $100 K		3	3	1.6 / 2.0	2.9 / 3.7	3.3 / 4.2
		4	3	1.7 / 2.2	3.0 / 3.8	3.4 / 4.3
0.10	0.90	1	9	2.0 / 2.6	3.2 / 4.1	3.6 / 4.6
MODERATE		2	3	1.4 / 1.8	2.8 / 3.5	3.2 / 4.0
• FOR FINDING MISTAKES IN 2 TO 3 DAYS • UP TO $500		3	2	1.4 / 1.8	2.8 / 3.5	3.2 / 4.0

However, a simple guideline for most comparative experiments in industry is to use an α risk of 5% (or a confidence of 95%) and then to select three B units and three C units. This gives one of the best balances between risk and the cost of experimentation.

Step 3: Randomize and conduct the tests.

As in factorial experiments, randomizing the sequence of testing, say, three Bs and three Cs, is mandatory. Randomizing filters out the effects of environmental factors, human bias, time of day, and other variables, so that the test results can be correctly attributed to an assignable cause—namely, the variable(s) altered from C to B. It is tempting, in production, to run three Cs with the existing process and then switch over to the B process. But that would defeat randomization, and the results could be invalid.

Step 4: Rank order the results.

Although ranking first requires measuring each B and C unit using a quantitative parameter, the ranking itself is qualitative— going only from best to worst.

Step 5: Decision Rule.

Based on the ranking, there are two approaches to a decision:

1. *The no overlap technique.* This is more properly referred to as a *no overlap end count.* In any ordered ranking of samples, the end count is that collection of either B or C samples that is unpolluted by samples from the other group. As an example, if there were three Bs and four Cs and the ranking were as follows,

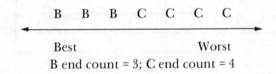

B B B C C C C

Best   Worst
B end count = 3; C end count = 4

There is no overlap; the B end count is 3; the C end count is 4; and the told end count is 7.

In the no overlap end count technique, no overlap of Bs and Cs is allowed. In the above case, the three Bs outrank the four Cs and so B is judged to be a better process, with 95% confidence (or with an α risk of 5% of assuming improvement when there could be no improvement). If only one or two Bs outrank the Cs, i.e., if there is overlap between the B and C rankings, B is not considered better than C and the decision will be not to make the change.

2. *The overlap end count technique.* In several industrial situations, it may be preferable to allow some overlap and still keep the risk

of wrong decisions very low. In this case, the *overlap end count technique* will be used. As an example, the ranking of five Bs and five Cs is as follows:

B   B   B   C   B   B   C   C   C   C

← ————————————————————————————————— →

Best   Worst

B end count = 3; C end count = 4; total end count = 7

Here, overlap exists. If overlap is to be allowed, the procedure (Step 2) changes slightly. The sample sizes for B and C are larger, generally ten or more for each, and equal. If they are unequal, the sample size for B, i.e., n_B, should be larger than for C, i.e., n_C. But the ratio of $n_B{:}n_C$ should be no more than 5:4. The larger sample sizes make the overlap technique slightly more expensive than the no overlap technique, but there is a resultant increase in sensitivity, in terms of a closer approximation to the population.

The decision rule for the overlap end count technique is based on the *6, 9, 12 formula*—derived from the same laws of permutations and combinations that were used to determine risks.

6, 9, 12 Rule

If n_B is equal to n_C or no greater than 20% larger, B is better than C when:

α Risk	End count is $\geq$
0.05	6
0.01	9
0.001	12

Step 6: Separate the means: The β Risk.

It is not enough, at the start of B vs. C testing, to determine only whether B is better than or the same as C (α risk). It is also important to determine, *a priori* again, the *magnitude* of the real improvement. The β risk is associated with this magnitude—separation of the mean (average) of B and the mean of C. The separation, or delta (Δ) distance, is measured in $K\sigma_C$ units, where K is a stipulated number selected by the experimenter before testing begins and σ_C is the standard deviation of the C process. (The B process may have too few

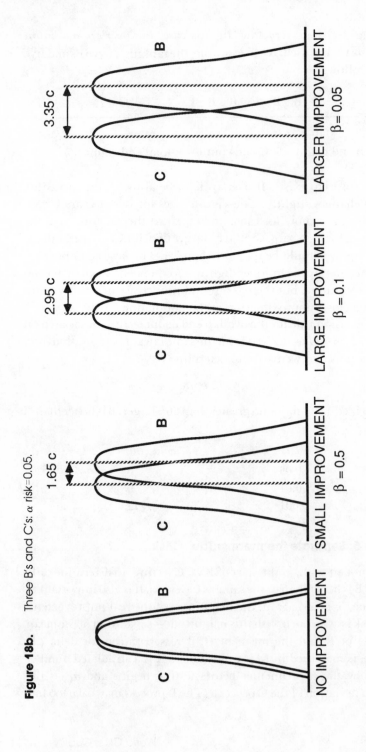

Figure 18b. Three B's and C's: α risk=0.05.

NO IMPROVEMENT

C B

SMALL IMPROVEMENT
β = 0.5

B C

1.65 c

LARGE IMPROVEMENT
β = 0.1

B C

2.95 c

LARGER IMPROVEMENT
β = 0.05

B C

3.35 c

units to determine an accurate σB^*.) Table 14 shows the K values for β risks of 0.5, 0.1, and 0.05. As an example, if one enters Table 14 with a α risk of 0.05, with three Bs and three Cs chosen as sample sizes, it indicates that for a β risk of 0.1, K should be 2.9. In other words, if the separation between the mean of B and C is at least $2.9\sigma_C$, then there is only a 0.1 (or 10%) probability that this improvement will go undetected. If there is larger improvement between the mean of B and C—3.5 σ_C or more—then there is only a 0.05 (5%) probability that such improvement will go undetected. The relationship between the separation of the B and C means and the associated β risks is summarized graphically below. (Assume $\sigma_B = \sigma_C$.)

3 Bs and 3 Cs: α Risk = 0.05

USES OF B VS. C

Even if the B vs. C tests indicate that there is no difference between the two processes in terms of quality, the B process can still be selected over the C process (or vice versa) if the B process is *less expensive* than the C process. (Of course, if the B process is worse than the C process in terms of quality, the switch to B should not be made.) Lowering costs is, sometimes, as valuable as a quality improvement.

As stated earlier, B vs. C is such a versatile tool that it can be used not only in engineering and manufacturing but in almost any field of human endeavor, where quick and easy comparisons can be made. This includes marketing, sales, advertising, human relations, forecasting, etc.

As an example, if a car manufacturer wishes to determine which of two styling approaches, B or C, is better, a quick and easy test would be to pick three typical customers and ask them, independently and separately, to indicate their preference for the B or C styling. If all three customers chose B over C, there would be a 95% confidence that the B styling was better. If there was no clear separation of B over C, the two stylings would not be perceived as significantly different. When either an improvement or an economic gain (with no improvement) is an expectation, B vs. C tests can be used for:

---

*In Table 14, the upper-case K values for the three β risks assumes that $\sigma_B \simeq \sigma_C$. The lower-case values for these risks assumes that σ_B is either larger or smaller than σ_C.

- Design/process/material changes
- Reliability evaluations
- Customer preferences
- Sales/marketing/service practices
- Sales promotions/advertising
- Human relations polices

B VS. C CASE STUDY: THE 64 K RAM

In the fabrication of a 64 K ram (semiconductor), a B vs. C test was run to see if standard substrates (C) in a room atmosphere could be produced in a high oxygen atmosphere (B) in order to improve yields. An electric parameter was chosen (not identified because of confidentiality). The α risk was chosen at 0.05 (5%) but the usual three Bs and three Cs were deemed to be an inadequate sample. Twelve C and thirteen B samples were selected and processed in random order. It was decided to use the overlap end count technique. The results were:

C

Standard   105.6, 102.5, 108.5, 114.6, 95.8, 88.3, 104.1,

Substrates   100.5, 97.5, 114.9, 103.7, 100.0
(room atmosphere)

B

High Oxygen   106.7, 101.2, 119.2, 108.6, 117.0, 109.4, 123.6,
Substrates   117.2, 114.5, 123.2, 99.3, 110.4, 118.2

The results were ranked in descending order as follows:

B 123.6 ⎫
B 123.2 ⎪
B 119.2 ⎪
B 118.2 ⎬   B end count = 6
B 117.2 ⎪
B 117.0 ⎭
C 114.9, C 114.6, B 114.5, B 110.4, B 109.4, B 108.6, C 109.5,
B 106.7, C 105.6, C 104.1, C 103.7, C 102.5, B 101.2, C 100.5,
C 100.0, B 99.3

C 97.5 ⎫
C 95.8 ⎬   C end count = 3
C 88.3 ⎭

Analysis. Total end count = 6 + 3 = 9. So the 6, 9, 12 rule is met, where for $\alpha = 0.05$, the total end count must be at least 6. Therefore B process is better than C process with 95% confidence.

PRACTICE EXERCISE ON B VS. C: THE TUNING COIL

A process change on a tuning coil was expected to increase torque, measured in inch-ounces. It was decided to list four C samples (current process) and four B samples (new process). It was stated that the proposed change would only be put into effect if all B samples outranked all C samples (no overlap).

All tests were run in random order. The results were (in terms of inch-ounces):

B 4.1, 4.3, 3.7, 4.2
C 3.6, 3.8, 2.5, 3.1

Question 1: What is the B end count? What is the C end count? What is the total end count? If there is overlap, what is its count?

Question 2: Based on the decision rule chosen (no overlap), what decision would be made about switching or not switching to the new process?

Question 3: If the decision rule chosen had been the overlap end count technique and an α risk of 0.05 had been selected, would the new process have been adopted?

These are the answers to the exercise on the uses of B vs. C.
Question 1. The ranking was as follows:

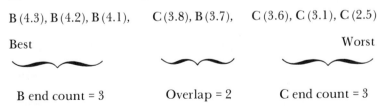

B (4.3), B (4.2), B (4.1),   C (3.8), B (3.7),   C (3.6), C (3.1), C (2.5)

Best   Worst

B end count = 3   Overlap = 2   C end count = 3

Question 2. Because the decision rule had been selected *a priori* as no overlap, the proposed change is *not* an improvement.

Question 3. With the overlap end count technique selected *a priori*, the 6, 9, 12 rule says that for an α of 0.05, the total end count should be a minimum of 6. The ranking shows a total end count of 6. Hence the proposed change does represent an improvement.

We can conclude that the above exercise shows the importance of selecting the α risk and the decision rule in advance of running the experiment.

Chapter 12

Scatter Plots: For Optimization and Cost Reduction

Scatter plots represent a graphical technique in which thirty readings of a range of values of an independent variable are plotted against the corresponding range of values of a dependent output. If there is a correlation between these two variables—a thin line or parallelogram—the independent variable is the Red X, and its most appropriate target value and tolerance can be determined. If there is little or no correlation, the independent variable is not important and its value and tolerance can be placed at levels that are the most economical.

APPLICATION AND PRINCIPLE

Scatter plots are used primarily for optimizing the levels of important variables rather than for problem solving. It follows multi-vari charts, variables search/full factorials, and B vs. C tests as the last tool to be used in the D.O.E. arsenal. It is a substitute for more sophisticated techniques such as evolutionary optimization (E.V.O.P.).

As with the other D.O.E. techniques, its appeal is its simplicity and its graphical, nonmathematical approach.

Scatter plot principles are best illustrated by the graphical sketches shown in Figure 19. Let us assume that the effect of an independent variable, X, upon a dependent variable, Y, is to be measured. An example would be the thickness of a medical filter as X and the fluid flow rate through that filter as Y. Thirty filters are measured for thickness and flow rates and the results plotted. If the plot is as shown in (A), there appears to be strong evidence of filter thickness directly affecting filter flow rate. As the thickness increases, the flow rate also increases proportionately. This is called a positive correlation. In (B), the correlation is not as strong. The same thickness seems to produce somewhat different flow rates. In (C) there is also a strong correlation, but the slope is negative. It means that as the thickness increases, the flow rates decrease proportionately. This is called a negative correlation. Finally, in (D), there appears to be no correlation. For the same filter thickness, there are widely differing flow rates.

Figure 20 is a further interpretation of scatter plots. It shows three independent variables, X_2, X_6, and X_7, affecting a dependent output, Y. Which is the Red X, the variable that most controls variation in Y? The novice might say that it is X_7, because it has the greatest slope. But the slope is dependent on arbitrary scales for X_2, X_6, and X_7. If the scale for X_6 were doubled, the slope would tilt downward to a flatter condition. *The Red X is the variable that has the lowest vertical scatter.* In Figure 20 it is X_6. One way to interpret vertical scatter is to draw a vertical line through the center of the ellipse that circumscribes the thirty plots. For a constant value of X it shows that Y has some variation—which, because X is constant, must be caused by all the other X variables. *Hence, vertical scatter is a measure of the total contribution to Y of all the variables added together, other than the particular X.* In Figure 20, X_6 has the lowest vertical scatter, followed by X_7 (a Pink X) and X_2 (a Pale Pink X).

PROCEDURE FOR DETERMINING REALISTIC TOLERANCES

1. Select the output (Y) to be optimized. Hopefully, the Red X, Pink X, etc., will have been pinpointed through the use of

Figure 19. Various scatter diagrams.

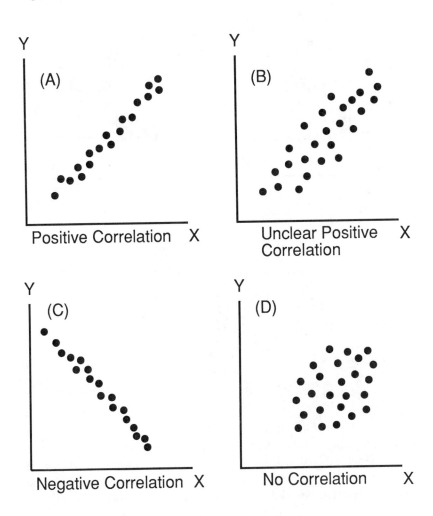

earlier D.O.E. methods such as the multi-vari chart, variables search and/or full factorials and confirmed with B vs. C tests.

2. Select a range of values for the Red X variable that is likely to optimize the output variable (Y). Run thirty such values of the Red X and note the corresponding Y values. Plot the results. If there is *tilt* in the graphics plot (the tilt need not be 45°, because the angle depends on the scale used for the Red X) and only a small vertical scatter, there is further validation of the Red X.

Figure 20. Interpretation of vertical scatter.

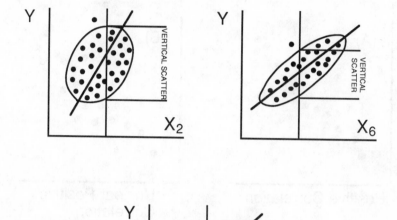

(See Figure 21). If there is no tilt, or the plot is a wide ellipse as in Figure 19 (D), the variable X is unimportant.

3. Draw a median line—called the line of regression—through the thirty plots. Draw two lines on each side of the median and parallel to it so as to contain all thirty plots. The vertical intercept through this parallelogram is the variation in Y due to all variables added together, other than the Red X. If this intercept is large (a fat parallelogram), the variable is a Pink X rather than a Red X.

4. If Y has a customer requirement, in terms of an upper specification limit and a lower specification limit, plot these points on the Y axis and draw two lines from them parallel to the X axis until the line from the upper specification limit intersects the upper line of the parallelogram and the line from

Figure 21.   Determining realistic tolerances with scatter plots.

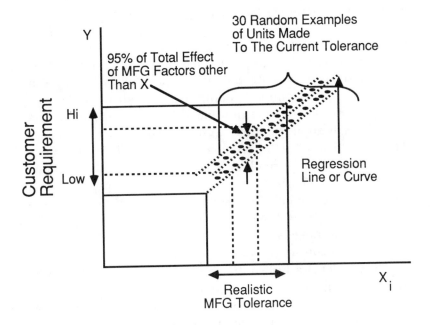

the lower specification limit intersects the lower line of the parallelogram. Drop two lines from these intersection points perpendicular to the X axis.

5. The horizontal intercept on the X axis between these two lines determines the maximum tolerances permitted for the Red X in order to assure conformance to customer requirements. This would assure a C_p of 1.0. Using precontrol rules, the horizontal intercept should be divided into four equal parts and only the middle half allowed as the preferred tolerance for the Red X. This assures a C_p of 2. Further, the target value of the Red X variable should be at the center of the horizontal intercept.

6. These correct target values and tolerances for the Red X should be compared against existing values and tolerances and the necessary changes made to assure zero defects and 100% yields.

REALISTIC TOLERANCES WITH SCATTER PLOTS CASE STUDY

In the fabrication of an engine ignition amplifier, production was experiencing a fairly high reject rate in a critical parameter—off-time—which determines the amount of time (in milliseconds) that the ignition is turned off in a rapid cycle of on-and-off switching. Previous studies had identified the Red X and Pink X respectively as R_3 and R_4 resistors. Figure 22 plots the range of R_3 and R_4 values.

The results show that R_4 was correctly identified as the Pink X. Its correlation with the off-time output is clear, but weak. The parallelogram is fat and the vertical intercept is about 60% of the total output specification width of 1.2 milliseconds (from 6 to 4.8 m.s.). This means that 60% of the variation is caused by all factors other than R_4. However, the plot graphically shows that the original resistance of 110 K ohms ± 10% was wrong and was one of the causes of the high reject rate. The maximum range should be from 94 to 102 K ohms, with the center value of 98 K ohms. This would assure a C_{pk} of 1.0. The optimum range should be from 96 to 100 k ohms (1/2 the tolerance) to assure a C_{pk} of 2.0.

The R_3 plot clearly identifies resistance R_3 as the Red X, with a thin parallelogram. The vertical intercept is only about 16% of the total output specification width of 1.2 m.s. (from 6 to 4.8 m.s.). This means that only 16% of the variation is caused by all factors other than R_3. However, the plot graphically shows that the original resistance of 120 K ohms ± 10% was wrong, leading to the major cause of the high reject rate of the ignition amplifier. The graph shows that the maximum range allowed should be from 118.5 K to 141.5 K ohms, with the center at 130 K ohms. This would assure a C_{pk} of 1.0. The optimum range can now be determined by the C_{pk} desired. If a C_{pk} of 2.0 is sufficient, the range would be from 124 K to 135 K ohms. If a C_{pk} of 4.0 is required, the range would be from 127 K to 132 K ohms. The final ranges should be based upon the desirability of achieving these values, balanced by economics.

PRACTICE EXERCISE ON SCATTER PLOTS: THE DIGITAL CIRCUIT

An output voltage in a digital circuit must be kept in the "on" or 1 condition to be considered acceptable. The "off" or zero condition is

Figure 22. Scatter plot case study: the ignition amplifier.

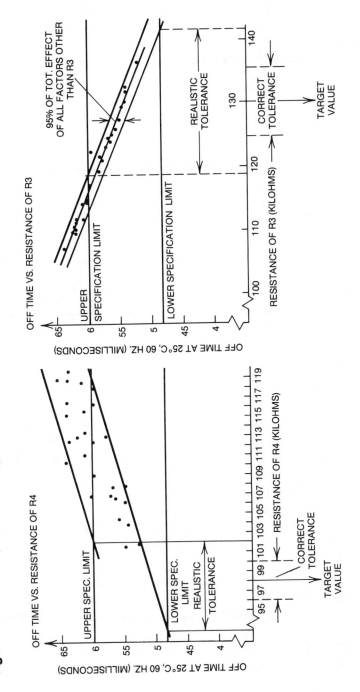

considered unacceptable. Previous studies of the circuit had identified a 1000 ohm resistor in the digital circuit as the Red X. Its tolerance was specified at ± 1%.

It was decided to check the validity of both the resistor value and its tolerance with a scatter plot shown below:

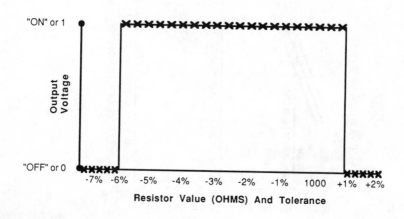

Question 1: Is 1000 ohms the right value? If not, what should be the target value for the resistor?

Question 2: Is the ± 1% tolerance right? If not, what should be the right resistor tolerance?

The answers follow.

Question 1: In this example, we are dealing with attributes— 1 : good and 0 : bad. So there is no tilt in the plot. The resistor at exactly 1000 ohms would give good results, but it is not centered. The center should be at a tolerance of 7%/2 = 3.5%, i.e., at 975 ohms.

Question 2: The tolerance could be opened up to ± 3.5%. However, that would only achieve a C_{pk} of 1.0. If the original tolerance of ± 1% is retained, the C_{pk} would be 3.5. In this example, if there is no great economic penalty in retaining a ± 1% tolerance, that would be optimum. If there is an economic penalty, the tolerance could be opened up to, say, ± 2%, but no more.

Part III

The March from Experimentation to Implementation

Chapter 13

The True Role of S.P.C.

Part II of this text has now clearly demonstrated that the systematic way to identify, analyze, and reduce variation is not through S.P.C. tools, such as control charts, but through the design of experiments (D.O.E.). What, then, is the true role of S.P.C.? *It is to maintain that reduced variation, to assure that it stays reduced at all times.* This is the only correct use of control charts—as a maintenance tool, not as a problem-solving tool. But, as we have seen in Chapter 2, precontrol should be a 100% substitute for control charts. There is nothing that control charts can do that precontrol cannot do—and furthermore do less expensively and with greater statistical effectiveness.

However, between the end of D.O.E. and the start of precontrol there are three disciplines that must be put into effect—positrol, process certification, and operator certification (see Figure 12).

POSITROL

One of the weaknesses of American industry is that its production engineers and technicians attempt to control a *process* by checking the *product* it produces. That is too late. A parallel, in nautical terms, would be to steer a boat by looking at the wake it produces! A process, like a product, has idiosyncrasies—inherent variables that must be identified and analyzed with D.O.E. tools. Chapters 9 and 10 offered examples of a systematic identification of process variables in a wave solder process and a drilling process. The important process variables were separated from the unimportant ones.

The role of positrol (a term meaning "positive control") is to assure that important variables ("the what"), identified and reduced with D.O.E. tools, stay reduced with a "who, how, where, and when" plan and log.

Table 15 presents such a positrol plan. The wave solder case study in Chapter 10 identified four process variables—flux, belt speed, angle of incline, and pre-heat temperature—as process parameters that needed careful monitoring to assure a 50:1 reduction in solder defects. The positrol plan determines *who* should measure these process parameters, *how* they should be measured, *where*—specifically—they should be measured, and *when* (how frequently) they should be measured.

Once such a positrol plan is prepared, its execution must be recorded in a log maintained at the process. It should be filled out by the designated person (who) and monitored periodically by the supervisor, process engineer, or quality control.

Table 16 is an example of a positrol log on a sputtering machine used to metallize glass, with a layer of chrome, nickel, and gold on one side of the glass, and chrome and gold on the other side. Previous history on the sputtering machine indicated continued "in and out" rejects for metal adhesion on the glass. The process engineer would "twiddle" one knob after the other in an effort to control adhesion, ending up "chasing his own tail" and becoming thoroughly confused as to what to do. D.O.E. experiments identified four factors— power, gas pressure, speed, and vacuum—as important, and established the maximum outer limits for each of these parameters. A log was then maintained by the operators four times a day on this three-shift operation. With D.O.E. and positrol, the rejects were reduced to zero!

In many cases, it is more economical to use precontrol, rather than a log, for process control. Precontrol has the advantage of being able to lengthen the period between checks on each process parameter if the time between corrections (two pairs of yellows) is comfortably long. In more modern processes, usually microprocessor-based, parameter tolerances can be designed into the process, such that positrol becomes automatic, eliminating the necessity for either a positrol log or precontrol. However, D.O.E. tools must be used first to

Table 15. Positrol plan for a wave solder process.

Parameter (What)	Specification	Measurement Who	Measurement How	Measurement Where	When
A 880 flux	0.864 gm./ cc ± 0.008	Lab. technician	Specific gravity meter	Lab	Once a day
Belt speed	6 ft./min. ± 10%	Process technician	Counter	Board feed	Each model change
Angle of incline	7° ± 20%	Process technician	Angle scale	Tilt post	Each model change
Pre-heat temp.	220°F ± 5°	Automatic	Thermo-couple	Chamber entrance	Continuous

separate important process parameters from unimportant ones and to determine the tolerances on each parameter, before microprocessor controls are designed.

Positrol is a simple, common-sense technique to maintain a process under control. Yet, it is amazing how infrequently it is used to monitor processes, even where S.P.C. has been widely used to monitor the products produced by these processes.

PROCESS CERTIFICATION AND MURPHY'S LAW

The humorous, but real, foundation of process certification is Murphy's Law—the universal adage which states: "If something *can* go wrong, it *will!*"

The major causes of variation—design, processes, materials—can be reduced with D.O.E. and maintained with S.P.C. But there are a number of peripheral causes of poor quality—scores of little Murphies lurking around the corner—that can negate and checkmate all these fine preventive measures. The immortal Murphy does not, however, constitute a prefabricated, all-purpose, fully exonerating excuse for shortsighted failures to attack and remove these peripheral causes of poor quality—each of minor importance by itself, but which collectively can spell quality disaster. The quality peripherals can be divided into three broad categories: systems, environment, and supervision. Table 17 presents a partial listing of various quality peripherals that must be investigated before a particular process can be certified to produce good quality.

Table 16. Positrol log.

PROCESS: METALLIZATION
MACHINE: 903
WEEK ENDING: 6-20-8?

MACHINE PARAMETERS		MONDAY				TUESDAY				WEDNESDAY				THURSDAY				FRIDAY				SATURDAY			
		6a	12p	6p	12a	6a	12p	6p	12a	6a	12p	6p	12a	6a	12p	6p	12a	6a	12p	6p	12a	6a	12p	6p	12a
POWER (W) 800-900	Cr	820	800	820	820	820	832	865	820	820	820	820	820	800	882	861	861	861	861	861	861				
47060-4900	Ni	4848	4830	4779.2	4779	4772	4772	4797	4779	4779	4779	4817.5	4817.5	4765	4772	4817	4770	4855	4855	4819.5	4819				
2300-2400	Au	2400	2400	2400	2400	2370	2370	2370	2510	2370	2370	2370	2370	2370	2370	2370	2340	2340	2340	2340	2340				
1050-1150	Cr	1066	1066	1066	1066	1066	1066	1066	1066	1111	1111	1127.5	1127.5	1127	114	1127	1127	1148	1148	1148	1148				
2300-2400	Au	2400	2400	2400	2400	2370	2370	2370	2570	2370	2370	2570	2570	2370	250	2370	2340	2340	2340	2340	2340				
GAS PRESSURE (μ) 3.0	Cr	3.0	3.0	3.0	3.0	3.0	3.0	3.0	3.0	3.0	3.0	3.0	3.0	3.0	3.0	3.0	3.0	3.0	3.0	3.0	3.0				
3.0	Ni	3.0	3.0	3.0	3.0	3.0	3.0	3.0	3.0	3.0	3.0	3.0	3.0	3.0	3.0	3.0	3.0	3.0	3.0	3.0	3.0				
9.5	Au	9.5	9.5	9.5	9.5	9.5	9.5	9.5	9.5	9.5	9.5	9.5	9.5	9.5	9.5	9.5	9.5	9.5	9.5	9.5	9.5				
9.5	Cr	9.5	9.5	9.5	9.5	9.5	9.5	9.5	9.5	9.5	9.5	9.5	9.5	9.5	9.5	9.5	9.5	9.5	9.5	9.5	9.5				
9.5	Au	9.5	9.5	9.5	9.5	9.5	9.5	9.5	9.5	9.5	9.5	9.5	9.5	9.5	9.5	9.5	9.5	9.5	9.5	9.5	9.5				
SPEED (IPM) 4.0	Cr	4.0	4.0	4.0	4.0	4.0	4.0	4.0	4.0	4.0	4.0	4.0	4.0	4.0	4.0	4.0	4.0	4.0	4.0	4.0	4.0				
7.5	Ni	7.5	7.5	7.5	7.5	7.5	7.5	7.5	7.5	7.5	7.5	7.5	7.5	7.5	7.5	7.5	7.5	7.5	7.5	7.5	7.5				
7.0	Au	7.0	7.0	7.0	7.0	7.0	7.0	7.0	7.0	7.0	7.0	7.0	7.0	7.0	7.0	7.0	7.0	7.0	7.0	7.0	7.0				
5.5	Cr	5.5	5.5	5.5	5.5	5.5	5.5	5.5	5.5	5.5	5.5	5.5	5.5	5.5	5.5	5.5	5.5	5.5	5.5	5.5	5.5				
7.0	Au	7.0	7.0	7.0	7.0	7.0	7.0	7.0	7.0	7.0	7.0	7.0	7.0	7.0	7.0	7.0	7.0	7.0	7.0	7.0	7.0				
VACUUM 3x10⁻⁶		3×10^{-6}	3×10^{-6}	3×10^{-6}	3×10^{-6}	3×10^{-6}	3×10^{-6}	3×10^{-6}	3×10^{-6}	3×10^{-6}	3×10^{-6}	3×10^{-6}	3×10^{-6}	3×10^{-6}	3×10^{-6}	3×10^{-6}	3×10^{-6}	3×10^{-6}	3×10^{-6}	3×10^{-6}	3×10^{-6}				
		3×10^{-6}	3×10^{-6}	3×10^{-6}	3×10^{-6}	3×10^{-6}	3×10^{-6}	3×10^{-6}	3×10^{-6}	3×10^{-6}	3×10^{-6}	3×10^{-6}	3×10^{-6}	3×10^{-6}	3×10^{-6}	3×10^{-6}	3×10^{-6}	3×10^{-6}	3×10^{-6}	3×10^{-6}	3×10^{-6}				
CHECKED BY																									
# OF RUNS AT END OF EACH SHIFT		12	14			10	9			5	9			7	8			9	8						

COMMENTS/PROBLEM CAUSE

Process certification starts with a checklist of various quality peripherals that must be evaluated. Not all the checkpoints listed in Table 17 are applicable in all situations. (Conversely, there are many quality peripherals unique to individual processes or quality systems that are not listed in it.) The checklist is usually drawn up by a process engineer and verified by a quality control engineer. Finally, a team—consisting typically of the process engineer, development engineer, quality engineer, foreman, etc.—physically examines a process or work station, and only when all the quality peripheral requirements are in place does the process get a "certification" to start production.

Periodically, the team must re-audit such a work station or process to make sure that variations from policy and sloppy practices have not crept back to cause potentially poor quality. It is recommended that such a recertification be conducted at least once a year. *If such certifications or recertifications were conducted on processes and work stations in the United States, 80% would fail even minimum requirements!* How can we build a superstructure of quality when these basic foundations are weak?

OPERATOR CERTIFICATION

As described in Chapter 4, operators are frequently blamed for poor quality when the real culprit is management. What quality can a worker be expected to produce when he is hired off the street and then give fifteen minutes of instruction by his supervisor? Training is the key word. This includes training, testing, certification, and recertification in ever enlarging circles so that the line worker of today becomes the knowledge worker of tomorrow. In Japan, operator training is an essential ingredient in its quality success story. Table 18 outlines the differences in operator training between the United States and Japan. In Japan, the line worker is trained so that, later, he can do the work of the technician; the technician so that he can do the work of the process engineer; the process engineer so that he can reach for the work of the design engineer.

Once D.O.E. has identified and reduced important variables, positrol has controlled important process variables, process certification has reined in quality peripherals, and operators have been certified, then and only then can S.P.C. be applied to the product, using precontrol as a powerful maintenance tool.

Table 17. A quality peripherals checklist for process certification.

QUALITY SYSTEM	ENVIRONMENT	SUPERVISION
. EFFECTIVE CONFIGURATION MGMT.	. WATER/AIR PURITY	. CLEAR QUALITY GOALS
. ENGINEERING CHANGE CONTROL	. DUST/CHEMICALS CONTROL	. CLEAR INSTRUCTIONS
. EQUIP./INSTRUMENT CALIBRATION	. TEMP./HUMIDITY CONTROL	. COMBINING TASKS
. PREVENTIVE MAINTENANCE	. HUMAN/PRODUCT SAFETY	. NATURAL WORK UNITS
. BUILT-IN EQUIP. DIAGNOSTICS	. LIGHTING/CLEANLINESS	. CLIENT RELATIONSHIPS
. VISIBLE, AUDIBLE ALARM SIGNALS FOR POOR QUALITY	. ELECTROSTATIC DISCHARGE CONTROL	. "OWNERSHIP" THRU VERTICAL JOB ENRICHMENT
. "POKA-YOKE" - FOOL-PROOF INSPECTION	. STORAGE/INVENTORY CONTROL	. FEEDBACK OF RESULTS
. NEIGHBOR & SELF-INSPECTION OVER EXTERNAL INSPECTION		. ENCOURAGEMENT OF SUGGESTIONS
. NO PARTIAL-BUILD POLICY		. COACH - NOT BOSS
. WORKER AUTHORITY TO SHUT DOWN POOR QUALITY LINE		

Table 18:   Operator training: United States vs. Japan.

U.S.	Japan
• Short, spasmodic, unfocused	• Long, continuous, geared to major strategies
• Little testing, certification, or recertification	• Testing and certification prerequisites for job and promotion
• No cross-training	• Cross-training for multiple skills
• Training practical, more on-the-job	• Training more in classroom
• Poor or no implementation of training	• Implemenation—the key
• No formal career plan for line workers	• Every worker has a management-by-objectives (M.B.O.) plan, with training as the means of achieving that career plan

Chapter 14

The Management of Change

Change is difficult for human beings. It is even more difficult for corporations. And it is a monumental task for nations, especially one like the United States, which still seems to be basking in the glow of past success. We seem to resist new ideas. Even when we accept them in principle, we feel that they may not be applicable to a particular company. And if that hurdle is crossed, we may not implement them, preoccupied as we are with fire fighting, bureaucracy, and just plain inertia.

The concepts and practices of D.O.E./S.P.C. outlined in this briefing present a special challenge because they require a *double* change—first, a change from traditional quality practices to the half-way house of traditional S.P.C.; and second, a change from traditional S.P.C. to the world of D.O.E. and meaningful S.P.C.

THE C.E.O. AS THE INSTIGATOR OF CHANGE

As with many other concepts, the adoption and *implementation* of the techniques described here must start with a company's chief executive officer (C.E.O.). He does not have to be an expert in the use of these techniques. But he must know that they exist. He must appreciate their simplicity, recognize their contribution to profitability and customer satisfaction, and feel their power.

The start could be exposure at a seminar. If these techniques can be understood by line workers, they can be grasped even more easily by C.E.O.s. Exposure should be translated into a set of quality axioms. These are:

1. High quality = low cost = high profitability = high market share = low absenteeism = low personnel turnover = high motivation.
2. Quality is a principal element of corporate strategy and a superordinate value.
3. In the march to world-class quality, D.O.E. and S.P.C. are the shock troops.
4. Defects can and should be outlawed.
5. The achievement of zero defects is only a milestone on the long road to zero variation.
6. Quality is redefined as the systematic identification, analysis, reduction, and eventual elimination of all variation around a target value, in order to maximize customer satisfaction, reduce cost, and enhance competitiveness in the marketplace.

Axioms, beliefs, and understanding should be translated into the following C.E.O. actions.

1. Seek out a D.O.E./S.P.C. goal champion from among the ranks of top management, who can become thoroughly immersed in these techniques and then pursue implementation as his sole responsibility because of the vastness of the payoff to the corporation. He then becomes the "process owner," the catalyst for change.
2. Make it mandatory for every technical person in the corporation to go through an intensive course on D.O.E./S.P.C. techniques. Lead by example, rather than by precept.
3. Establish a management steering committee to monitor progress. The use of workshops, as a follow-up to seminars, is particularly useful. Here teams bring in D.O.E. solutions to chronic problems that have sometimes plagued the company for up to three years. Learning by doing is infinitely superior to learning by listening.

4. Measure progress by the number of D.O.E. projects undertaken. Calculate the dollar benefits to the company from quality improvement, cost reduction, and cycle time reductions. Review one (or two) projects in detail, so that it can provide a suitable training ground for the C.E.O.'s own expertise.

ROLE OF THE DESIGN ENGINEER IN EFFECTING CHANGE

The design engineer—both for the product and for the process—is the principal "hands-on" instrument for change. It is he who will:

- Hear "the voice of the customer"—i.e., determine the customer's needs and expectations.
- Determine a target value associated with each product specification and design to such target values rather than to broad specification windows.
- Use D.O.E. techniques to greatly reduce variation at the prototype stage and during engineering and production pilot runs. (The design engineer should not use full production or the field as an extension of the laboratory to solve problems.)
- Establish product and process compatibility—not by designing processes as mere afterthoughts to fit frozen product designs but by using a product-process interdisciplinary team approach.
- Translate important product parameters into component specifications using D.O.E. techniques (i.e., specify high C_{pk}s for the truly important component specifications while opening up the tolerances on all other component specifications to reduce costs).

THE SUPPLIER'S ROLE IN EFFECTING CHANGE

To a large extent, a positive change in supplier responses to D.O.E./S.P.C. is the responsibility of the customer company. It must reduce the supplier base and promote a partnership with the supplier, so that the latter can, in effect, become an extension of the customer company. It must educate the supplier's management. It must train the supplier's technical personnel in D.O.E./S.P.C. It must help solve the supplier's chronic quality problems through the use of D.O.E. tools.

For his part, the supplier should:

1. See that top management follows the same prescriptions outlined for the customer company's C.E.O.
2. Have his design engineers follow the same guidelines enumerated for the customer company's design engineers.
3. With encouragement of the customer company, get involved very early in the design of the part he is to produce, so that his ideas and expertise can be utilized in determining part requirements. This is known as early supplier involvement (E.S.I.), a practice that is an absolute requirement of the supplier partnership philosophy.
4. Achieve high C_{p_k}s for each of his processes, using D.O.E. tools.
5. Maintain these high C_{p_k}s with the use of positrol, process certification, and precontrol and submit precontrol charts to the customer company as proof of excellent quality.

PRODUCTION MANAGEMENT'S ROLE IN CHANGE

As with the C.E.O., the change in production management must start with a set of production quality axioms. These are:

- The line worker will perform as a highly motivated individual—unless "ground down" by poor management with a bossy attitude or forced to work in an atmosphere of fear.
- The line worker's brain is as fertile as management's, given training, encouragement, and support.
- Inspection and test add no value to a product and should be drastically reduced.

To successfully implement D.O.E./S.P.C., production management must:

1. Drastically reduce fire fighting quality problems in production by insisting that every important quality characteristic on every new product entering production (at the pilot run stage) be measured for process capability—a minimum C_{p_k} of 2.0. (This can be quickly ascertained in an approximate manner by

the precontrol rule of five units in a row falling within the green zone.)

2. Establish positrol, process certification, and operator certification as ironclad disciplines.
3. Maintain reduced variation with precontrol, not control charts.
4. Encourage the concept of the next operation as customer (N.O.A.C.).
5. Measure progress:
   - *The cost of poor quality: external failure and internal failure and appraisal.* Strive for these costs to be well under 2% of sales.
   - *Yields: defects per unit (D.P.U.).* Add up all defects at all workstations and divide by the number of units shipped. Strive for a maximum of 0.01 D.P.U.
   - *Cycle time.* Measure clock time for one unit to go through the plant from one end to another. Strive for a maximum cycle time of no more than twice direct labor time. (This is called theoretical cycle time.)

QUALITY MANAGEMENT'S ROLE IN CHANGE

Because many current quality practices are obsolete, this requires as large a metamorphosis in the role of the quality professional as in that of the C.E.O. or production management. He must:
- Become an absolute expert in D.O.E. if he is to be of real value to his company.
- Change from being a "policeman" to a teacher, consultant, and coach.
- Assist the goal champion in prioritizing areas to attack and problems to solve, and cooperate in interpreting results and measuring progress.

THE MARCH TO WORLD-CLASS QUALITY

None of the D.O.E./S.P.C. techniques described in this briefing are rooted in a *national* culture. It is only an industrial culture that needs to be changed. Can U.S. management effect that change? It is not easy for the mightiest nation on earth, which has taught the principles of quality to the rest of the world, to admit that it too must now learn. But the greatness of America is that it is always willing to hold up a mirror to itself, to engage in self-criticism, to analyze, and to improve. In the past, the nation has often shown an amazing resiliency and single-minded purpose in moments of crisis. With that upbeat, can-do, buoyant spirit, we shall **OVERCOME!**

About the Author

Keki R. Bhote is the senior corporate consultant on quality and productivity improvement for Motorola, Inc. His research contributions include work in such areas as statistical design of experiments, total cycle time reduction, benchmarking, and supply management. His previous position at Motorola was group director, total quality of performance, where his responsibilities extended beyond product quality control into all areas of improvement, including productivity, inventory reduction, and profitability.

Mr. Bhote received a B.S. in telecommunications engineering from the University of Madras and an M.S. in applied physics and engineering sciences from Harvard University.

He is author of *Supply Management: How to Make U.S. Suppliers Competitive*, published by the American Management Association, and co-author of *Value Analysis Methods*, published by Hayden Publishing Company. His next book, an in-depth treatment of supplier quality assurance initiatives, will be published by the American Management Association in 1989.

Mr. Bhote serves as associate professor at the Illinois Institute of Technology, where he teaches courses in quality control, reliability engineering, and value engineering. He is also a seminar leader for the American Management Association. In addition to lecturing extensively on three continents (the Americas, Europe, and Asia), he has published numerous papers and has addressed many professional societies. His most recent concentration is a study of Japanese management and quality practices that can enable the U.S. to meet the Japanese challenge.

Mr. Bhote was chosen as one of the Ten Outstanding Young Men by the Junior Chamber of Commerce in Chicago and one of six Outstanding Naturalized Citizens of Chicago by the Immigrant Service League. In 1970, he received the Zero Defects Award from the U.S. Department of Defense. In 1975 he was recognized by the United Nations Association for distinguished services to the U.N. In 1978 he was listed among the "Community Leaders and Noteworthy Americans" by the American Biographical Institute. In 1982, he was listed in *Who's Who in the Midwest* and in 1984 he was listed in *Who's Who in Finance and Industry.*